THE JOSEPH PRINCIPLE

Published by RS Walker Enterprises
DBA Mentoring & Real Life Coaching
2768 Crain Highway
Waldorf, Maryland 20601
Office (240) 573-3418
Web address: http://www.rswalkerenterprises.com
For Products: www.bishoprswalkerproducts.com
E-mail: admin@bishoprswalker.com

ISBN-13:
978-0692494615

ISBN-10:
0692494618

Published in the United States of America

Dedication

This book is dedicated to my lovely wife Pastor Betty A. Walker. She has been an extraordinary blessing to me and provides tremendous support with all of my writing projects. Her encouragement and assistance, in every area of preparation is greatly appreciated.

Thank you Betty! I could not do this without you.

Acknowledgements

Thank you to my sons, Rodrick Walker, Rodney Walker Jr and Kelly Putman for your contribution in developing the book cover. To Elder Iris Young for your contribution with formatting and organizing. To Lisa Burges and Pualette Walker for your contributions with editing. To Lashawn Dobbs, Iris Young and Elder Cynthia V. White for your support and assistance in preparing the book for publication. I appreciate your willingness to meet the challenges necessary to prepare this product for printing and distribution. To my son, Rodney S. Walker, Jr., Pastor Cathleen D. Moore and our entire hardworking team of Prophetic Presbyters for all of their contributions on this project.

Thank you to all of my students at Bishop R. S. Walker Ministries School of the Prophets for the great questions and demand you cultivate which assist in developing me as a Prophet. Your ideas and suggestions contributed immensely to the success of this project. It is good to have all of you as part of the team. I am confident that good things will come from our joint efforts. There is no way I could get this project completed by my efforts alone. Thank you again for a job well done.

Appreciation

I would like to take this opportunity to thank Fruit That Remain LLC, Publishing and Nikki Robinson for your support and assistance in the preparation of this book for publication. I appreciate your willingness to meet the challenges of transcribing tapes to the final preparation for printing and distribution. Your ideas and suggestions contributed immensely to the success of this project. It is good to have you as part of the team. I am confident that good things will come from our joint efforts. Thank you again for a job well done.

Contents

CHAPTER ONE

You Are Part of the God Class

Your Creative Nature and Authority

Let's begin in the Book of 1 Thessalonians. I want to share things that are truly important. 1 Thessalonians 5:5-10 reads, "Ye are all the children of light, and the children of the day: we are not of the night, nor of darkness. Therefore let us not sleep, as do others; but let us watch and be sober. For they that sleep in the night; and they that be drunken are drunken in the night. But let us, who are of the day, be sober, putting on the breastplate of faith and love; and for a helmet, the hope of salvation. For God hath not appointed us to wrath, but to obtain salvation by our Lord Jesus Christ, Who died for us, that, whether we wake or sleep, we should live together with him."

As we think about the things that God has done in our lives and is doing in our lives now, we need to zero in on, capture, and take a look at things in this passage that move us toward destiny and what God is saying in this particular season of our lives. Look at this passage that we so often use as a latter day passage to talk about prophecy and things to come. I want us to look at this from a whole different viewpoint than before. 1 Thessalonians 5:1-5 reads, "But of the times and the seasons, brethren, ye have no need that I write unto you. For yourselves know perfectly that the day of the Lord so cometh as a thief in the night. For when they shall say, peace and safety; then sudden destruction cometh upon them, as travail upon a woman with child; and they shall not escape. But ye, brethren, are in darkness, that that day should overtake you as a thief. Ye are all the children of light, and the children of the day; we are not of the night, nor of darkness."

One of the things that I think we need to see in this is God's view of us as the people of God. When God looks at you and me, he is looking at somebody whom he does not view as an individual of darkness. Nor does he look at you and me as individuals who are of the night. When God looks at us as a people and as the body of Christ, he looks at us as people who are of the day—that nothing sneaks up on us, that nothing just takes us by surprise. This is tremendously good because he says in the first verse, "In regards to seasons and times you don't even need me to talk to you about that."

A New Way of Operating

Why is it that the church of Thessalonica didn't need him to talk to them about seasons and times? Here is the number one reason: they were recognized as a church that had matured in areas of life where they had exercised their senses, and they understood seasons, they understood times, and they understood that they had arrived at a point where they didn't need to hear things about those subjects. When God looks at us, he checks to see that we are mature in the things of God. When he looks at us, he wants us to understand that we are in the God class.

Now often times this is not how we really think of ourselves. We don't think of ourselves in the God class. We think of ourselves as being "less than" We think of ourselves as people who may not come up to the mark of God. As we begin to focus on what God is saying and what God is doing inside us, here is how we have to view this: God looks at us as being in his class.

In Genesis 1:26, which begin, "And God said, Let us make man in our image, after our likeness: and let them have dominion over the fish of the sea..." God says; let us make man in our image and after our likeness. Let them have dominion over the fish of the sea, let them have dominion. God looks at us as being in his class. God looks at us as being people of authority so we can carry out his assignment in the earth. God expects you and me to carry out whatever he would do as if he were actually here. 1 Thessalonians 5:5 says "Ye are all the children of light, and the children of the day: we are not of the night, nor of darkness." We have to get to the point where we absolutely, wholeheartedly understand exactly the kind of people that we are. One of the reasons that we don't produce on the level at which God expects us to produce is that we don't really understand who we are. God has actually made us on his level at his class, but he is saying because of that I want you to have dominion on the earth, and I want you to have dominion over everything that I set on the earth.

When we understand this, and if we really receive this, he says, "Here, the exact place where I created Adam is the place where I want you to stand." David asked the question about this in Psalm 8:4, "What is man, that thou art mindful of him? and the son of man, that thou visitest him?" David was having a problem identifying with God in the way that he made man.

My question to you is if God made us that way, then why is it that we are minimizing ourselves in our thought process as to how or what we could do? God how can you use me, or God, why do you even want to use me? I know you have never asked God that. I know you have never had those kinds of thoughts, God bless you, but you know some of us have had those kinds of thoughts. But understand that when God was looking at us, he gave us a particular assignment. He didn't look at you and me as if we were "less than." He looked at us as if we were in his class. In Philippians let me show you this a little further. We are going to come back to this, but I think maybe we need to try to prove a few things because we might not really understand that this is the actual way that God sees things. Philippians 2:5-8 reads, "Let this mind be in you, which was also in Christ Jesus: Who being in the form of God, thought it not robbery to be equal with God: But made himself of no reputation, and took upon him the form of a servant, and was made in the likeness of men: And being found in fashion as a man, he humbled himself, and became obedient unto death, even the death of the cross."

I want to ask you a question. Do you see yourself in the God class? Do you really see yourself in the God class, or do you see yourself as somebody who can't compare to or align with who God is even though it was God himself who made you in his image and after his likeness? I want to educate you to the point where you will start to produce at the level of expectation. Understand this: most of us do not produce at the level of God's expectation for us. We have to expand our thinking because where we are in the level of our operation at this particular time is nowhere near how God really sees us. So if God sees us in the God class, then what hinders us from operating in that class? What hinders you from operating at the level where you operate right now? What hinders you so you don't operate as an individual in the God class?

Let me tell you about a problem that I have. There was a time I didn't like reading instructions. I think I can figure it out, and so getting something to operate at its fullest potential took me a little longer because I didn't like to read the directions. Once I was messing around with my car's navigation system. You know what? I have a whole book in my glove compartment.

My instruction book looks brand new, and the car is old now. So I was messing with the navigator one day and searching through the menu. Now mind you, for two years I wanted to know the whole route; I followed the blue line all the way down through the whole thing. You know, if I had read the book, if I had read the directions, it would have told me that there is a button on the menu side that you can push and sit back and watch the whole thing as it takes you from beginning to end. But I didn't want to read the book, so it took me two years to find it out. Well, I am about ready to get rid of the car now when I could have enjoyed that feature. There are features about ourselves that we could have enjoyed for 30 years, but we couldn't enjoy them because we have never read the Book. We have never figured out how we are supposed to operate.

Many times we argue with the Book based on what it says that we can do and who it says we are. I was listening to one of Les Brown's messages one day, and he was talking about what he said to his brother. His brother jumps out of planes, but when it comes down to earning money his brother couldn't see doing what Les does. And so Les tried to increase his brother's potential by teaching him some things that he knew, but his brother argued with him, "Well, you know Les, I can't do that." And this stuck in my thinking; Les replied, "Stop arguing with me, because if you argue about your limitations you get to keep them." If you argue regarding your limitations when God is saying you can excel far beyond where you are right now, then you get to keep those limitations.

You must understand that you are part of the God class. If you can believe that, you will do much more than you are doing right now. In Genesis 1:26, "And God said, Let us make man in our image, after our likeness: and let them have dominion over the fish of the sea…" Now it gives you a whole list of things you have dominion over.

Drop down to verse 27-28, "So God created man in his own image, in the image of God created he him; male and female created he them. And God blessed them, and God said unto them, be fruitful and multiply, and replenish the earth, and subdue it: and have dominion…" All of this is what God has placed in our makeup.

God placed inside you the ability:

1) **to be fruitful** - How you think. The word, "Fruitful" is a primitive root; to bear fruit (literal or figurative):- bear, bring forth (fruit), (be, cause to be, make) fruitful, grow, increase.

2) **to multiply** - What you do with your thoughts. The word "Multiply" is a primitive root; to increase (in whatever respect) :- [bring in] abundance (× -antly), + archer [by mistake for <H7232> (rabab)], be in authority, bring up, × continue, enlarge, excel, exceeding (-ly), be full of, (be, make) great (-er, -ly, × -ness), grow up, heap, increase, be long, (be, give, have, make, use) many (a time), (any, be, give, give the, have) more (in number), (as, be, be so, gather, over, take, yield) much (greater, more), (make to) multiply, nourish, plenty (-eous), × process [of time], sore, store, thoroughly, very.

3) to replenish - Refill things that are depleted. The word "Replenish" is a primitive root, to fill or (intransitive) be full of, in a wide application (literal and figurative) :- accomplish, confirm, + consecrate, be at an end, be expired, be fenced, fill, fulfil, (be, become, × draw, give in, go) full (-ly, -ly set, tale), [over-] flow, fullness, furnish, gather (selves, together), presume, replenish, satisfy, set, space, take a [hand-] full, + have wholly.

4) to subdue - Don't be passive. The word "Subdue" is a primitive root; to tread down; hence negative to disregard; positive to conquer, subjugate, violate: - bring into bondage, force, keep under, subdue, bring into subjection.

5) to have dominion - Take Authority over things. The word "Dominion" is a primitive root; to tread down, i.e. subjugate; specifically to crumble off :- (come to, make to) have dominion, prevail against, reign, (bear, make to) rule, (-r, over), take.

… Whatever it is that you are doing right now, I want to ask you this all important question: Are you fruitful in what you are doing right now? If you are not fruitful, why aren't you fruitful? Most of us come up with excuses, such as, that is something that a certain person hasn't taught me. Why give that person that kind of power over your life? That person will limit you, but God has given you the ability to be fruitful.

A Fruitful Lifestyle

Fruitfulness has nothing to do with how much you have in the bank; it has nothing to do with how many cars you have or how many houses you have. This is where the deception comes from. Satan puts deception out there for us because he knows we will receive it and believe it. So fruitfulness has to do with what you have in your head that you actually pursue by way of goals and dreams. If you are not fruitful in your thinking, you are not going to manifest anything much in your world.

Do you understand that? Do you have some needs in your life? You may have some financial needs. Do you need some money? I am not going to turn this into a workshop, but if you need some more money, then why is it that you don't get the more money that you need? Let's back up to your ideas, dreams and aspirations.
Do you have any ideas or dreams that you could put into action that will get you some more money? Now I am not talking about what you are doing right now, but do you have any ideas, dreams or aspirations? If you do, then you are displaying fruitful traits. You don't necessarily end up in a manifestation, but you have to start with a fruitful capacity.

Multiply Your Millionaire Status

Now understand this: Each and every one of us has millionaire status even if we don't ever reach it. But most of the time we don't move on everything that we have or think about. Most of us never push ourselves to the level of producing what is next. We are fruitful, but what is next? Multiply! Somewhere between fruitfulness and multiplication needs to come a process of developing what is in your mind right now. I am fruitful, but how do I get fruitfulness out of my thinking and into manifestation? I have to multiply what is inside of me and get you to do the same.

You can be fruitful, but if where you are not hurting you badly enough, you are never going to move up. Either you are going to go in the direction of your pain or you are going to go in the direction of your comfort. Most of us will get away from pain and move toward comfort, but if you don't know that you have the capability of developing that comfort, then you know what you will do? You will keep lying right on the nails because you think that is as comfortable as you can get. Talk to yourself and say, "I'm going much further than where I am because where I am has me locked in." You are the only one who can remove the lock from the door because the lock is not on the outside. The lock is on the inside, so you are the only one who can remove it.

The first step is to be fruitful, and the second step is to multiply. God put the ability within you, so you cannot say that you don't have it.

My wife and I were watching a movie the other night and it challenged my thinking. I don't know why God does that to me. You know, he let me watch the movie, but there was one thing they said in the movie, and I didn't get any more of the movie because I couldn't get past that part. The movie was over for me; we were still sitting there watching, but the movie was over for me. The movie was the "Shawshank Redemption," and the character named Brooks hung himself. But before he hung himself, he put a knife to one his friend's throats and slightly cut his throat because Brooks was being released from prison the next day, and then the character played by Morgan Freeman said, "You don't understand him, he has been here for fifty years. He has been in this prison for fifty years and knows nothing but this. He doesn't know anything else outside of these four walls where he has been all these years." Morgan Freeman proceeded to say "He is institutionalized. It means he lived in this one place all this time and didn't know how to function outside of that prison. Many of us have been institutionalized also based on our institution and environment. When God starts to talk about being fruitful and multiplying, replenishing, subduing, and having dominion, we don't understand what he has been talking about because of the institution that we have been living in all of this time. And so when God says you can do it, we have no clue what "it" is. The thing that keeps us institutionalized is the fear of breaking out.

Look at yourself in the mirror and say, "Self, you have to take a risk." Most of us are institutionalized based on where we have lived all this time.
We get to the point where we don't realize that we all have some area of our lives in which we have been institutionalized, and we are scared to break out because this is all we know.

What is it that could possibly block us from our possibilities? It is all surrounding that fear because we would rather go back to Egypt, to what we are familiar with, as opposed to going to a land that flows with milk and honey that we are not familiar with. I don't know that I am going to be able to make it over there, so let me go back to slavery. Look at yourself and say, "Self, break out." Now here is the thing that we have to understand: It is in us—being fruitful, multiplying, replenishing, subduing, having dominion—it is in us. Regardless of where you are locked in, you always at least think, even if you don't meditate on it, about the possibility. Most of our possibility is based on the fact that God is talking to us about it. We have to look at it to tell if it is a fear. Sometimes we are scared to stay in, and so it is a fear that tries to push us out. Then sometimes there is a fear to break out because where God or that inner voice has for us to go is based on what he already spoke to us about. God said he has already told you what you would be, he has already told you what you would become, and he has already told you what you would have, but you are scared to move to the next level.

The ability to multiply is in you. When you function properly as part of the God class, there are particular things that you just go ahead and do. You understand what needs to be done and you do it. You don't spend time arguing with yourself. You know what the God class is all about—the people who will understand what needs to be done and do it. I refuse to let God say all that I am and not at least move toward coming into some of that myself. Peter would have never been able to preach on Pentecost if he hadn't jumped off the boat.
He had to jump out onto a surface that didn't even look stable. I mean, just get out of the boat, Peter. None of the rest of them was qualified to preach on Pentecost; you have to show that you have enough guts to go for it.

I am a member of the God class. Understanding that I am a member of the God class, I am fruitful, I'm a multiplier, and I'm a replenisher. What does that mean? I am a replenisher. I can go into (and you can go into) what is empty and what has been cleaned out and replenish it. I wonder how many of us would be able to look at what is not working, design a plan, and make it work again. As a member of the God class, that is in you. The next part of being in the God class is having the ability to subdue some things. Once you have been fruitful and have multiplied and have replenished, you are going to have to subdue some things, so you cannot be passive. If you are passive, people will take advantage of what you have.

Subdue or be Replaced

I like to think of the word "Subdue" in terms of "bringing something into subjection. If you are going to prosper in areas of life, business or even family you will have to develop and "Subdue" things that attempt to get out of order or unruly. There is a favorite quote I have that I like to use, it says "Until the pain of staying the same, becomes greater than the pain to change you won't." What that means is you have to bring into subjection anything in your life that becomes unruly. When bad habits, addictive ways, people that mishandle your business or just slothful employees that are not functioning properly and bringing things down you can't stand by and not bring it under 'subjection". Remember this, God does not give abundance to bad managers, therefore if we act as if we cannot handle what God gives us, he will give it to someone else who will manage it well. If you don't believe me, ask Adam.

God had to kick Adam and the Woman out of the Garden because they did not "Subdue" the Serpent that got out of order and got them to question God's authority. When Aaron and Miriam questioned Moses God's anointed vessel God brought that under subjection quickly.

Dominion Is a Principle of Life

Now for the fifth part of being in the God class, we have to have dominion; we have to be one who exemplifies dominion. Have you ever walked into places where the people look like they are in charge, but aren't? I was at the medical center yesterday, and the staff at my doctor's office didn't do what they were supposed to do. Here I was at this medical center, and these folks still didn't have my paperwork. So you know I had to realize, boy, you are from the God class, because when I called, they said, "The person that you need to talk to is not here right now." Now I was standing at the desk at the medical center and they were saying, "Sir, the person that you need to talk to is not here right now. Her name is such-and-such, and I am going to put you in her voicemail, and she will get back with you when she gets back from lunch." I said, "That is not good enough. It has been three weeks and my paperwork should have been over here. You need to get it done now." What was I doing? I was exercising dominion. I have dominion—I have something invested down at that doctor's office. If you are passive, you just go ahead and be put in the voicemail. If the doctor's office had been put in the voicemail and didn't get any results, then you won't get any, either. And so you have to subdue, which means that you are not going to be passive in this. Even though you may bear that characteristic of being a passive person, you are not going to be passive right here.

I'm only pointing out to you that you need to be somebody who is going to exercise dominion, or folks will come and use up all of your stuff; they will take advantage of everything that you have built up to this point. God is having us build some great things, some great businesses, and some great visions. God will have you build things that are designed to bring you the harvest that God talked to you about. Then after you have built that thing that is designed to bring in your harvest, you know what happens next? People come and start to tear down what you have built.

Now let's discuss the characteristics of the God class people. Back in 1 Thessalonians 5, verse 6-7, "Therefore let us not sleep, as do others; but let us watch and be sober. For they that sleep sleep in the night; and they that be drunken are drunken in the night." Verse 8 says, "But let us, who are of the day, be sober, putting on the breastplate of faith and love; and for a helmet, the hope of salvation." You have got to be sober; you have to be alert. There are things that God want to do for us. He wants us to design, but the only way that we are able to do this is to wake up from our sleep and become alert. That means that nobody owes you anything. Young people, this is one of the things that you are going to have to get, because understand this, God wants to do things for us, but do you understand that no one owes us anything? What this means is if you want to do something—I know you guys have dreams—that means that you have to go out and make it happen and keep God first. Nobody owes us anything. Some of us are sitting idly by waiting on something to happen as if somebody is going to bring it by and drop it in our laps. It's not going to happen that way. You have to be fruitful, you have to multiply, and you have to replenish. You can't use anybody as an excuse for not developing what God puts into your mind. (Well, Lord, I couldn't get them to work. So what? Somebody will work.)

Not only do you have to do that, but you have to be watchful and focused. What breaks our focus? We can't afford the luxury of having people around who break our focus because we have to make sure it is what God said that he wants us to do. Why? We have so many things around. Do you realize the Devil doesn't have any problem with your working for the Lord? He just doesn't want you to be doing the thing that the Lord told you to do. So you have to be sober, meaning alert. Why? So that we don't miss an opportunity. When an opportunity presents itself, you need to be ready to jump, and if you are focused as soon as it shows up, you know that it is a part of what you are supposed to be doing.

Right now my wife and I have our eyes and our hearts set, and we are looking for properties—not just any property that arrives, but for the properties that we are supposed to have in this season. Not every property in this season is what we need to handle right now. There could be some properties in this season that we are dealing with that could wipe us out and give us a setback. Do you know what we are looking for right now? We are looking for a quick sell and a must sell, because we may not be able to depend on what has been sustaining us to continue to sustain us. It means that you have to reach into your faith-filled vehicles that are designed to bring your finances and make those things work. If you don't make them work, then you go down, and you can't afford the luxury of what is going to cause you to go down. For example, in order for your attention to be focused on a million-dollar property that is going to bring you $2,000,000, you might need to pay for $100,000 worth of work on it, and it may take you out—that's good vision but bad focus. Let's reduce the amounts. Maybe we are not going to be able to make that $1,000,000 overnight, and so what are we going to do?

We are going to look for a $50,000 property that we will gain $100,000 from and that we don't need to invest any more than $10,000 in, and we will build up to that $1,000,000 property. You might say your interest is not in that particular area. Apply it wherever your area is, but know that God has put it in you; that is all I am saying. You are of the God class.

Get Prejudices out of Your Life

You also have to be of faith and love; you absolutely have to walk in the love of God. Within love there is no room for prejudice. They can't make you be prejudiced; they can only present you with an opportunity you make the decision of whether or not you flex those prejudice muscles. No, I'm not flexing them. I have some other muscles that I want to flex, muscles of faith. You can't flex muscles of faith and prejudice at the same time. How do you know whether or not you have that prejudice root working inside yourself? Here is the only thing that you have to do. Turn on a boxing match. If you root for your kind, you know there is still a prejudice root somewhere inside you. You don't know either one of the boxers, but somehow you just automatically like him. You know they are coming around the track field, black and white. How do you know you have some prejudice left? Because you don't know neither one, and the one whom you are pushing along is the one who is your kind. If you want to get that prejudice out of yourself, on purpose root for the other one who is not your kind. Isn't it amazing that in most of our churches we have a black Jesus hanging somewhere? You visit people's homes and they have a black Jesus. Come on now, you are prejudiced. You have to walk in faith and love because the only way we are going to get God's work done is to walk in love. Faith doesn't work without love. You might think, Well, I did everything; I followed it all the way through. Well, was there anybody that you operated out of love with?

You might say that it doesn't matter, but it has everything to do with your success in doing God's work; you have to be walking in love. The test comes at this particular season, when God is trying to tap us into millions, and it is a distraction. I have asked the Lord to give me a root canal in every area of my life where I need it. If you leave the root in there, it will come back up. Get the root out. When your harvest starts growing, you don't need the root to pop up.

Last is the hope of salvation. I wonder how many of us really have the hope of salvation. I didn't say the hope of going to heaven; salvation means more than going to heaven. In my salvation I have experienced going to heaven, I have experienced the fullness of prosperity that is locked in my salvation, and I have experienced divine health and divine healing, which are both in my salvation. All of that is in my salvation—walking in the righteousness of God, the integrity of God—all of that is in my salvation. Having the hope of salvation means that having the hope of all of that. Just being saved is not enough anymore; you have to have more. Why? God promised more. The very hindrance to the opportunity that God wants to give us to bring in his harvest is that you may not be walking in the hope of salvation. I am going to keep on repeating this until I think that everybody has heard it.

If your job—your main source of revenue—went down, what do you already have that is still working that will produce that same level of revenue or more? If your answer to that question is nothing, you are in bad shape because most of us do not know the length of time that that position would hold. But what do you have that is still working? Remember that God has made us fruitful so there is something that God has told you that you can put into place that is designed to bring you the level of revenue that it takes for you to operate in your life and more.

It is there. Move back into focus. We have to focus on exactly what it is going to take to get that running for God.

Creating Multiple Streams of Income

Ask, Father, what is it going to take to get that running? Sometimes it is a business. It very well may be a ministry; it doesn't have to be a ministry, but it may be a ministry. Everything that is designed to bring revenue is based on two things: products and services that you could put into place because you are fruitful. What could you put into place that would generate what you are already bringing in and more? What could you offer? God wants to absolutely make us wealthy beyond our wildest imagination, particularly if we can handle it. Now that doesn't change his wants; he still wants to see whether we can handle it or not, but now the revenue is going to be based on products and services.

In my life the number one vehicle according to the will of God is products and services from Bishop RS Walker Ministries and conferences, workshops, books, tapes, CDs, and DVDs. What this means is that after the preaching is over, no one wants the preacher any more. Do you know what people want? They want information that they are going to be able to follow, that they are going to be able to use as a guide to put some things in place that are going to move them from where they are to where they need to be. In the same way of thinking, based on products and services, what can you offer that is going to bring about revenue that is going to equal what you are already making or more? Bishop RS Walker Ministries is not just about me as an individual. The books, tapes, CDs, and DVDs are our products, and the conferences, church services, workshops, training sessions, and retreats are our services. But that is only one vehicle that God has given me. I had to get to the point where I didn't focus on that alone.
On the other hand, if you have ten vehicles you might really focus only on the main three so you can do those well.

I am sharing God's plan for me, just a portion of the plan. The second vehicle in God's plan for us is called KING: Kingdom Investment Network Group, a real estate investing company that we are putting together that is designed to tap into a level of revenue through buying and selling real estate. We have already begun. By the end of this month, the house that my wife and I just bought is going to be worth at least $100,000 more than what we paid for it, so we can sell it, move out, and do what we need to do. Our Waldorf property, by the time we get that to the point where we need it to be, will be worth somewhere between $70,000 and

$90,000 more than what we paid for it, so if we want to sell it to purchase another property, we can repeat the process.

Understand this: we have to have a plan in place. This is something that God has given us to do; I can show you in the Bible. But you have to jump from where you are and take a risk. I'm not telling you to quit a job; there is faith, and then there is foolishness. But from where you are right now, you can put a strategy in place to increase beyond where you are.

CHAPTER TWO

Three Dimensions of Operating

I was in a worship service one day, the Lord revealed some insights about worship or intimate time alone to me. This is what was revealed. Sometimes worship leaders move into worship, and if you are an individual who spends a great amount of time worshipping, sometimes it doesn't take you any time at all to get into that place of worship where you sense God's presence or just receive ideas. But the Lord made me notice that some people are incapable of following the worship leader into a place of intimacy with God. Sometimes when worship leaders shift so swiftly into worship many worship leaders are not conscious of the fact that some people aren't able to follow them into worship.

As we think about this, we have to consider whether we are at a place in our lives where we are able to easily go into worship, or whether we are able to just be satisfied with praise, or whether we even deal with those areas. Maybe we don't praise him or worship him at all. Maybe we just merely exist. So I asked the Lord's permission to write on the subject because I believed that maybe I could get everybody to go into worship time alone or thinking sessions together. Sometimes we don't consider whether other people are ready to follow us into those moments; we are just kind of there.

So I want to talk to you about being people of the God class, find time alone or just having thinking sessions. I believe that it is imperative that we understand and know exactly who we are and that we are people of the God class/His Creation.

We are people upon whom God has put his spirit, we are people whom God has ordained to do a particular thing, we are people whom God wants to walk with him, and he with us. He wants to talk with us and wants us to talk with him. God has a desire to introduce us to: new ideas, witty inventions and creations. Many times we don't understand that God wants that kind of relationship with us.

One writer writes, "When I consider thy heavens, the work of thy fingers, the moon and the stars, which thou has ordained; What is man, that thou art mindful of him? and the son of man, that thou visitest him? For thou hast made him a little lower than the angels, and hast crowned him with glory and honour. Thou madest him to have dominion over the works of thy hands; thou hast put all things under his feet: All sheep and oxen, yea, and the beasts of the field; The fowl of the air, and the fish of the sea, and whatsoever passes through the paths of the seas. O Lord our Lord, how excellent is thy name in all the earth!"

David was a man that God from time to time could really brag on, and David was a man who I believe really understood worship or intimate time alone. He understood praise. He understood when to worship and when to praise or just be alone with Him. Now we begin to zero in on some things that God began to talk about. First of all, what is man that God is so mindful of him? What are we, who are we, that God is so mindful of us that he would give us his absolute attention without distraction? God is saying, "You know that I really want to have relationship with you." Think about the fact that God wants to have a relationship with us. Revelation 3:20 reads, "Behold, I stand at the door, and knock: if any man hear my voice, and open the door, I will come in to him, and will sup with him, and he with me." God is saying, "Look, I want to have relationship with you badly, but at the same time I am willing to only come in if you will let me in."

So when I began to think about the people who were not able to move into worship, it occurred to me that sometimes we require people to worship God when they have no ability to worship him. Can anybody worship God? Yes, they can if they have ability to do so. But not everybody has the ability to do it. By the time we get done with this chapter you are going to be able to say exactly where you walk with God—whether or not you are actually walking with God in the intimate place or whether you are in a process struggling to get in there. We don't just walk into relationship with God. It would be wonderful to walk right into relationship with God, but we don't. We can have relationship with God, but the intimacy that all of us could enjoy we don't enjoy.

Understanding Who You Are

Let's look at Genesis. Who are we that God should be or that God is so mindful of us? Exactly who are we? David found out that not only are we the people of God, His personal creation, His earthly management team, but that God is so committed to who he is to us that he will put all things under our feet, and he has made us to have dominion. Find someone that will keep you accountable and say to them, "God has made us to have dominion." However, we also need to understand this: Our ability to have dominion is one of the reasons that it is difficult for us to submit to other people. Because we know that God made us to have dominion, it becomes difficult to absolutely submit, and so then God has to tell us to submit to one another. Submission is not necessarily an easy thing, so God provides a process by which we can do it.

Remember that the only time anything is hard is when you transgress against the thing that seems hard. Here is something powerful.

I was listening to a man of God who dropped this into my spirit as I was listening to his CD, "You have to know the rules of the relationship that you are in. Every relationship has rules, and if you don't know the rules of relationship, regardless of the kind of relationship it is—it could be a spousal relationship, it could be a work relationship, it could be a relationship with your brother or sister, it could be a team player relationship, it could be a business relationship, it could be a ministry relationship—whatever kind of relationship it is, the relationship has rules, and so when you transgress the rules it is hard. But that is the only time it is hard.

Really think about it. What was your hardest moment in the relationship between you and whoever you are in the relationship with? The hardest moment was when you did what the other person didn't want you to do. When you broke a rule, friction came into the relationship. So if we know the rules of the relationship, then we will know what to do and what not to do, and we can take difficulty out of the relationship. God said that the way of the transgressor is hard. God is the one who gave that revelation. He says, "Look, if you want difficulty to leave, stop being a transgressor." Look at yourself and say, "Self, if you want difficulty to leave, stop being a transgressor."

Now that we understand that every relationship has rules, then we should also understand that in our relationship with God it would behoove us not to transgress the relationship. In other words, it would behoove us to ask, "God, what are the rules in the relationship? Okay, Father, I realize that you want me to get all the way from the outer court (where all normal people exist) to the Holy of Holies (where process makes you different), so it means that I am going to have to understand rules of the relationship in order to get there."

The First Dimension

Through every dimension there is a process. All of us have started right at the first dimension (where all normal people exist), where there is absolutely no worship and no praise because there is no relationship there, nothing to challenge you to be different. We are coming to a point where we are establishing relationship with God. We have to come in through the gate of the outer court, where there is also the brazen altar where your sins (areas of compromise) are burned up. Think about this. God has placed everything under your feet; all things are under your feet. So God has set you in a place with him that says that everything is under your feet. So when you come through the outer court, past the brazen altar, you can't get through unless you lay your sins (areas of compromise) down and let God burn them up. So everything in the first dimension is consumable, which means that you can't hold onto anything that you value in that dimension because when you hold onto that you are holding onto that which God is going to burn off anyway. In the first dimension, where are your values? What kind of values have you held dear to your heart in the first dimension?

God is trying to actually get us to the third dimension, but what we have to understand is that we don't get to the third dimension without going through a process. Here is the process: In the first dimension we come through the gate of the tabernacle, we stop by the brazen altar where our sins are laid and burned up, and we move from there into the Holy Place (the second dimension). Let's go back to the first dimension. Right beneath the altar we see the word "wood;" this

is where your stuff gets tried in the fire and gets burned up. In the second dimension, the Holy Place, the only things that exist are gold and wood.
That means that in the first dimension there is no relationship with God, in the second dimension where there is gold and wood, what you actually have is flesh versus spirit or spirit versus flesh and this is where there is a war going on.

We have to understand that when we live within the scope of our operation, we are going to understand that, but then we are going to understand what we have to do in order to move into the next dimension. If you are living the first dimension life, you can't stay there because God is trying to burn all of that up. Read Genesis 1:26-28: "And God said, Let us make man in our image, after our likeness: and let them have dominion over the fish of the sea, and over the fowl of the air, and over the cattle, and over all the earth, and over every creeping thing that creepeth upon the earth. So God created man in his own image, in the image of God created he him, male and female created he them. And God blessed them, and God said unto them, Be fruitful, and multiply, and replenish the earth, and subdue it: and have dominion over the fish of the sea, and over the fowl of the air, and over every living thing that moveth upon the earth."

God wants us to do five things in Genesis 1:28: be fruitful, multiply, replenish, subdue, and have dominion. He says, "Look, I am creating you in my image. If you are going to live like God class people, you are not going to be able to stay in the first or the second dimensions." God is provoking us to grow up. We can't stay in the first dimension because everything in the first dimension is consumable and will be consumed by fire. In the first dimension, the outer court, what we have going on there is total flesh. It is there that we did what we wanted

to do, we said what we wanted to say, and we went where we wanted to go. We did all of that because we were living in the first dimension.
But then it took commitment to come out of there; we realized that God was demanding something of us that the first dimension couldn't produce. In the second dimension, which is flesh versus spirit, here is where I want you to go now.

Today we are going to have to be transparent and we are going to have to be honest with ourselves. If we are honest with ourselves, we will have to admit that there is a battle going on between our flesh and our spirit; our spirit is insisting that we do one thing, and our flesh is insisting that we do something else, so there is a battle going on in this second dimension.

Now let's just assume that we have all come out of the first dimension. We don't want to say what negative thing that comes to mind, we also don't want to do the first thing that comes into our thinking, we don't want to do all of those things, and so we have made a quality decision that we were going to press beyond what we were accustomed to. We were going to press beyond our environment and move into the Holy Place. But now the problem is that most of us get stuck right there. Remember that starting out with wood tried by fire brought us into gold and wood. In the Holy Place, there is only gold and wood. The things that are there are also partially consumable; there are some good things in there, but there are a great deal of things that are going to burn up. So there are still things that you cannot take into the Holy of Holies. And so now from there into the Holy of Holies you are going to experience another level of being tried in the fire. But by the time we get to the Holy of Holies, the third dimension, there is nothing in there consumable. Everything is pure gold.

The Second Dimension

The second dimension is where most Christians operate because we don't want to make a total commitment to anything. Total commitment means we want to keep some level of say-so or control. In Revelation 3 I want to show you this, because now once we really see this, then we are going to understand that statement is actually true. In Revelation 3:18-19, we read, "I counsel thee to buy of me gold tried in the fire, that thou mayest be rich; and white raiment, that thou mayest be clothed; and that the shame of thy nakedness do not appear; and anoint thine eyes with eyesalve, that thou may see. As many as I love, I rebuke and chasten: be zealous therefore, and repent."

This leads us to believe that this passage is not directed at unsaved folks, but the next verse, Revelation 3:20, says, "Behold, I stand at the door, and knock." Talking to folks who are saved, he says, "I am not knocking at the door of the sinner, I am knocking at the door of saved folks." If we are in relationship with him, he shouldn't have to knock at the door. And since we have him knocking at the door, there are areas in our life that we have not opened to him. And because he is a gentleman, he won't just come in. For instance, God has to knock on the door to get us to tithe sometimes because our money is off limits to him. But if we operate in the third dimension, our money or anything else is not off limits; he is in there.

Let's go back to Romans now because I want to show you there is a battle going on in the second dimension. In the second dimension we are experiencing the battle between flesh and spirit.

Your spirit wants to do a particular thing and your flesh is opposing it, and then your flesh wants to do a particular thing and your spirit is opposing it. You have to be very honest with yourself, and you are going to have to identify the things that are flesh versus the things that are spirit. Let's talk about something that happened in the first dimension in your life and in my life, where we have not come to a rich place of understanding. Now just because you had a thought does not make it God's, and just because you have a thought doesn't make it yours. In the first dimension, we got damaged because we were so flooded with thoughts that we didn't originate; they came straight from the Enemy. So once we step into the second dimension, we must determine whether each thought is our thought.

The Third Dimension

This is what blocks us from getting into the third dimension. Let's say a thought has come; the thought is not yours until you verbalize it. I want to prove that this is absolutely wholeheartedly correct. 2 Corinthians 10:3-5 reads, "For though we walk in the flesh, we do not war after the flesh: (For the weapons of our warfare are not carnal, but mighty through God to the pulling down of strong holds;) Casting down imaginations, and every high thing that exalteth itself against the knowledge of God, and bringing into captivity every thought to the obedience of Christ…."

What that says is that the fact that a thought came to you doesn't mean that it is yours. So before you verbalize it, take that thought captive and throw it down. But once you have actually signed on the dotted line of that thought, it is yours.

How do you sign on the dotted line of a thought? You verbalize what you thought; you verbalize what came to your mind.
But it is in the mind's realm that you are going to have to identify what belongs to you and what doesn't. So stop tolerating stuff that just comes in your thinking that is not yours. Remember, if we are going to enter into third dimension, we are going to have to be able to trail right behind God.

God wants us to understand that he is not satisfied just that we made it to the third dimension. The third dimension makes us happy, and it means that we have a spirit-led life. But with a spirit-led life, the spirit of God is in front of us, and we are trailing right behind him and following his every plan. Ephesians 3:20 says, "Now unto him that is able to do exceeding abundantly above all that we ask or think…"What this says is that when we go beyond the church, there are things that God doesn't have to say because we are now trailing behind him; we are doing like Enoch, walking with God. Look at yourself and say, "Self, I want to learn to walk with God and not just behind him."

When we start to live this way, we have to accept that we are marked as one who is different from others in the church. They may ask why you do all of this stuff totally differently from everybody else. Many times people are just alike in the church because they don't dare to be different. They don't dare to do what God really wants and move beyond.

In Revelation, as God was speaking in the church, John had to look back to see the voice that spoke in the midst of the seven golden candlesticks. But John had transcended the church. He had moved past the church so that at this particular point, being with God, he had to look back to see where the voice was coming from. He was moving in the third dimension; this is the reason that he could be on the Isle of Patmos on the Lord's Day and remain in the spirit.

Either we can be happy with the first dimension or the second dimension, or we can decide that through the process we are going to move through the veil. The veil is designed to keep you from knowing some things if you are refusing to transition from second to third dimension. On the other hand, the veil is designed from the third dimension to reveal some things. We have to move through the veil to move into the third dimension. A mystery is only a mystery to those who are not there. It is information that is hidden from you but revealed to us. I guarantee you that there is much that God has been trying to get us to know, but we have been blinded by the veil. There is a war going on. What blocks us from being able to get into the third dimension from the second? Remember that in the first dimension, you do what you want to do, you say what you want to say, you go where you want to go, and all of that. That is just the life that we have lived. But in the second dimension you had to start monitoring the things that you have said, the places you have gone, and all of that. You had to start monitoring those things, but in the third dimension they don't exist. In the second dimension, the reason the flesh and spirit battle is that you still have a will; you have not surrendered it. If we are ever going to enter the third dimension, we will have to surrender our will because there is no place for our will in the third dimension.

I have had times like this. I don't know whether this is normal or not, but as it pertains to ministry, sometimes people ask me if I get tired. The fact is that I have never thought about whether I am tired. Most of the time I find out that I am tired when I go to bed and my head hits the pillow. Because I have given my will over to do God's will, my thought process is not, "Rodney, you are tired, you don't feel like doing this." Anytime somebody says, "I don't feel like it," we know that they are living somewhere in the second dimension. We already know that because we feel it. But in the third dimension, the only thing that registers is "What did God say?" Nothing else matters.

Adam started out in the third dimension, and there Adam and God walked in relationship through the garden in the cool of the day. When God said that partaking of the tree meant that Adam would surely die, Adam didn't physically die, but he ceased to exist in the third dimension. He went back to the first dimension because he had sin that had to be burned up. He didn't die physically; he just ceased to exist where he was. Now understand this that is all Adam knew. Think about this—nothing else existed. The second dimension didn't exist, and the first dimension didn't exist as far as Adam was concerned. All he knew was himself and God. In the same way, before Jesus came to earth that is all that Jesus knew. So all Adam knew was the presence of God and that God was his father. He had no will to do anything else but serve God and to be part of the God class. But then Adam partook of the forbidden fruit and ceased to exist in that dimension. Just think about this. All of a sudden he was zoomed into the first dimension in the outer court. Now when you have lived in the absolute presence of God, how do you even survive in the outer court totally out of the presence of God to the point where you just do what you want to do, no chastisement in the outer court? So we have to make the decision. Where do we want to walk? Do we want to walk in the absolute presence of God, or are we content with the second dimension to the point where there is always a battle going on flesh versus spirit, spirit versus flesh? These are contrary one to another.

Romans 7:7-8 reads, "What shall we say then? Is the law sin? God forbid. Nay, I had not known sin, but by the law: for had I not known lust, except the law had said, Thou shall not covet. But sin, taking occasion by the commandment, wrought in me all manner of concupiscence. For without the law sin was dead."

Romans 7:15 reads, "For that which I do I allow not: for what I would, that do I not; but what I hate, that do I." Can you identify with this at least a little bit? "I hate it, but I still do it." The battle of spirit against flesh is going on. But you don't have to stay there; remember that in the second dimension there are levels leading you to the Holy of Holies. If you are staying as close as you can under the table, then you are a little on the warm side, but you are really almost cold. But it starts to get warmer the closer you get to the Holy of Holies, which means the price starts to get a little more tremendous as you start to get over there. Because by the time you move through the veil you are going to have to have a made-up mind that you want to go in there, and you don't want to ever come back out. This is what we have to decide.

I am going to be the first one to tell you that as you are moving in that direction it is not an easy fight because you still have some will left. In the battle between the spirit and the flesh, the spirit is trying to push you toward the third dimension, and your flesh is trying to prevent you from going. Your total flesh is in the first dimension, and there is still a strong pull on that side. But the closer you get to the third dimension, the more that stronghold starts to weaken. Then you reach the point where you have to be absolutely willing to let go of your will, saying, "God, I turn my will over to you."

There is a trying that takes place once you say that. When the struggle starts to take place in that second dimension, it is at this particular point that we absolutely, wholeheartedly have to kill whatever it is that still belongs in that first dimension. Although you can bring some things along into the second dimension, by the time you get into the third dimension, all of that has got to be gone. In other words, we have to get to the point where we are just absolutely willing to say, "God, not my will."

When Jesus said, "God, not my will" in the garden of Gethsemane, it was at that point that he died. His first step was right there, so the cause was not a problem. He hung upon the cross for about six hours nailed to a tree, both feet together and hands and feet hanging by a nail. His body weight probably 160 to 180 pounds hanging from three nails. He said, "I thirst;" Psalms 22 says that his tongue was like sun baked clay, his mouth was tremendously dry, but yet when he cried out, he cried out with a loud voice. Something is wrong with this picture; he was tremendously thirsty when most of us would have been dead before we got to that point because our will to live would have left us. But then he realized he had to hand over his mother to somebody who could take care of her, the one who was closest to his heart and had the most compassion. Then he had to reach the point of saying, "It is finished," and then he had to reach beyond the point to hand over his spirit to God. Jesus had to do all of that, so he could not develop a will to die until then. So he got all the way through, and then yelled out with a loud voice. How did he yell out with a loud voice after going through all of that?

Let's come back down to where we are and ask how Jesus didn't develop a will to die even though everything wasn't done. He had only a will to do the will of God the Father, as in the third dimension. But we scream and holler in the second dimension because we still have a will. We holler even more than that in the first dimension; as a matter of fact, we get physical in the first dimension. Mess with me if you want, but you had better make sure I'm not in the first dimension. Love is very conditional in the first dimension, but when we get into the second dimension, we start to have a little more grace and mercy on us, a little more kindness. And in the third dimension we only have a will to do the will of him that is in us. So we don't develop a will to die before it is time in that dimension because our whole life is in the hands of God.

How is it then that we get from one dimension to the next dimension? There is only one way: we have to develop a life of worship. You can't worship only once a week at church on Sunday. It is not going to happen that way because once we have developed a life of worship, we are on the bus worshipping God and problems start coming. You don't jump out of the spirit to deal with the problem; you stay in the spirit to deal with that problem. It takes a process to deal with moving beyond that veil. You are not going to move beyond that veil without the process. What is it that you are going through right now that is part of your process that you are willing to just absolutely do away with?

God called you before the foundation of the world. Before the creation of the world, he knew exactly what you would be and who you would be. Remember you were preordained to be who you are, and therefore he started out long ago to develop you to be that. So you make the decision, because you are living in the second dimension where your will is very much alive. You have to kill your will. Look at yourself and say, "Self, I am a person of the God class."

God wants us as a people to come to a greater level of operation and a greater level of being productive. This is one of the things that we want to make sure that we are doing. It is extremely important for us to understand that God wants us productive. Look at yourself and say, "Self, God wants you productive." We should understand that God has no problem with our being productive; as a matter of fact, he expects and insists that we be productive. I believe that church shouldn't be just what we have been known to call church in the past. I believe that we have to understand that church is a meeting place to bring us to a higher level of operation, whether physical, natural, or spiritual. God wants us to operate from a whole different standpoint than from where we have operated so far. Genesis 1:26-27 says, "And God said, Let us make man in our image, after our likeness: and let them have dominion over the fish of the sea, and over the fowl of the air, and over the cattle, and over all the earth, and over every creeping thing that creepeth upon the earth. So God created man in his own image, in the image of God created he him, male and female created he them." Now look at the plan of God as it pertains to us as his people. Genesis 1:28 says, "And God blessed them, and God said unto them, Be fruitful, and multiply, and replenish the earth, and subdue it: and have dominion…."So not only was God expecting for us to be fruitful, but also to multiply, to replenish, to subdue, and to have dominion.

If we really understand that this is how we are supposed to operate, then our whole mindset changes, and even our level of expectation changes. What is it that we are expecting to happen on our part? I was listening to Les Brown one day, and he said something that absolutely amazed me. He said that the hardest thing in the world for him to do was not to make a million dollars, but to believe that it could happen to him. Think about that. If having a million dollars is possible, could it happen to you? Try to honestly believe it could happen to you. If we really believe that, then why do some of us expect it and why do some of us not expect it?

Whatever happens to us normally happens at the level of our comprehension. Let me say that again: Whatever happens to us normally happens at the level of our comprehension. If you can comprehend its possibility; then your mindset is geared towards understanding that it is *going* to happen, not just that it *can* happen. If we believe that it can happen to us, then we within the spectrum of its ability to happen to us, we need to go into motion to make things happen.

We have to start expecting things. The Bible says that faith comes by hearing and hearing by the Word of God. If we want faith for a thing, it means that we need to talk about it. Look at yourself and say, "Self, if you want faith for a thing, you need to talk about it." The more we talk about it, the more faith comes. Regardless of whether we are dealing with a spiritual situation, a physical situation, a mental situation, or other situation, if we can hear about the thing, then we start to gain faith for it. And nothing is really going to happen apart from faith. What really is faith? Faith is your believing that you receive exactly what God said that you can have.

We have to understand what God is expecting of us. Genesis 1:28 says, And God blessed them, and God said unto them, Be fruitful, and multiply…."So these are two of the things that God expects from us. Fruitfulness does not have anything to do with what you possess; fruitfulness has to do with your mindset. We see people who come into large sums of money automatically, and their money always dwindles down because of their inability to handle it. You might experience this when you get paid. Let's check you out about four days later. For some of you, it doesn't take four days. After four days, what is your level of being able to handle what is put into your hands?

How does God really view this? On our chart of dimensions, it depends on your level of thinking according to whether you are in the first dimension, the second dimension, or the third dimension. What is the level of your thinking? Are you thinking in an area of total flesh, flesh versus spirit, or a spirit-led life? Exactly which area are you thinking from? If you are thinking out of the area of total flesh, your productivity is going to be down because that kind of a person will turn out to be totally materialistic, with more liabilities.

If you came into a million dollars right now, I wonder what you would do first. Would you buy a house? Would you buy a car? Most of us know a car is a liability. As soon as you drive it off the lot because it loses some of its value it is a liability. So the last thing that you want to do is get the car. What I have found in this type of situation is that we actually do stock up on liabilities as opposed to gaining assets. If I were to go to a drawing board and draw two columns, one marked "assets" and one marked "liabilities," I guarantee you that the majority of people would be in trouble based on the board because we have tremendous numbers of liabilities but very few assets. What is an asset? An asset is something that is going to increase in value in the assets column. However, a liability is something that is going to decrease in value and subtract from your assets column.

So what do you have that is going to produce over and over for you? Think about this. I'm not expecting you to start to naming things, but what do you have that is going to add value to you like that? God has made you and me fruitful. How many of you believe that what God says comes to pass? Let me show you once again what God said. "And God blessed them and God said unto them be fruitful and multiply, replenish, subdue, and have dominion." God said all of those things, and what God says happens.

The problem comes in when we don't cooperate with what God said. He said to the earth, "Light be," and the light came on. He told the firmaments where to be, and he separated the waters so there was water above and water beneath. Did it happen? Yes. But when he tells man be fruitful, multiply, replenish, subdue, have dominion, then we don't cooperate.

What is the difference? The difference is when God spoke to the earth, earth had no will, when he spoke to the firmament, firmament had no will, but when he talked to us he has given us a will. Look at yourself and say, "Self you have set your will."

When I was disabled, I set my will to be healed, but at first it wasn't set. I had to set my will to be healed because God told me that he already healed me, but by way of manifestation I wasn't healed. But by way of the Word and the will of God I was healed. And so getting that out of the spirit realm where he said that I was healed I had to set my will that it would be manifested. Any area that you set your will is a guaranteed manifestation. I am talking about the power of agreement with God. If you set your will, it is a guarantee that you will manifest exactly what you set your will to do or to receive, because God has already said that.

Have dominion over what? Let's go back and look at it because I am telling you it comes down to this. When it came down to my getting healed, I had to know just like that. Because when the Devil confronts you on it, and he will, you are going to have to know that God said that I am healed right now; he says right here in this Word. Genesis 1:28 says again, "And God blessed them…" God was not going to bless them. Look at yourself and say, "Self, God is not going to bless you; you have already tapped into all the blessing that you are ever going to get." You have already tapped into as much of it as you are going to get, you are never going to get more blessing than you are right now. You are not going to tap into more. If you are going to get more, where are you going to get it from when the Blesser has already blessed you?

Genesis 1:28 says, "And God blessed them, and God said unto them, Be fruitful, and multiply, and replenish the earth, and subdue it: and have dominion over the fish of the sea, and over the fowl of the air, and over every living thing that moveth upon the earth." And Genesis 1:26 reads, "And God said, Let us make man in our image, after our likeness: and let them have dominion over the fish of the sea, and over the fowl of the air, and over the cattle, and over all the earth, and over every creeping thing that creepeth upon the earth." So if it is in the earth, you and I have dominion over it because you are blessed and God has already blessed you. Because God has already done it, then there is nothing more that is going to happen. So you know what you have to do. If God has said that, then you need to set your will on it.

When it came down time for me to get healed, I had to set my will on that. The plan of the Enemy was to have me as a cripple, but it was up to me to set my will on it. I was disabled, was collecting on disability insurance, and the whole scheme of things. What really got my attention was when social security sent me a letter saying that if I didn't sign it, it would only lead them to believe them I wasn't really disabled. And I thought, God has called me to preach faith, and my signature would have indicated to all of heaven, all of earth, and everything under the earth that I was what they were calling me. My signature would have meant that's it; the final step that needed to have been taken was putting my signature on it. I am trying to tell you exactly how powerful your signature is. Your signature doesn't only mean that you are signing in the natural world. God recognizes your signature because when you sign, then God holds you to what you signed.

What it means to subdue and have dominion is that you can't be passive. You can't passively receive anything.
The Bible says that the violent will take it by force, which means that you can't be passive in this because the Devil is not going to allow you to come into it if you are passive. You have to boldly stand on the fact that God said I could have it, and it is mine right now in Jesus' name. Let's go a little further with this. We have to understand exactly which area we are operating out of because remember we are people of the God class, and when God created us he created us in his image and after his likeness, we had the ability to do exactly what Jesus did. Why? We are people of the God class. In other words, we are to think like God. Have you ever thought that God wants you to think as he thinks?

Philippians has one of the most important scriptures that we will ever come into contact with. Philippians 2:5-6 says, "Let this mind be in you, which was also in Christ Jesus: Who, being in the form of God…" Remember how God created us? He created us in his image and likeness. It speaks to his form and it says that this is the form of God. Let's read Philippians 2:5-7, "Let this mind be in you, which was also in Christ Jesus: Who, being in the form of God, thought it not robbery to be equal with God: But made himself no reputation, and took upon him the form of a servant…."

Most of us don't take the form of a servant. We may look at ourselves as if we are servants, but we weren't born servants. Look at yourself and say, "Self, I was born in charge." But he took on himself the form of a servant, "Who, being in the form of God…" You are of the God class, so you are in the form of God and so being in the form of God he took upon himself the form of a servant because he doesn't look like a servant.

Look at yourself and say, "Self, God doesn't look like a servant and that is the reason I don't." But he took upon himself the form of a servant.
Even though you don't look like it, and even though you look like you are in charge, you take upon you the form of a servant because God at least wants to see that you are willing to serve so that he will know that you can lead effectively but you look like you are in charge, and you are supposed to look like you are in charge.

Have you ever really thought about the number of people who criticize other people who look like they are in charge? You know what they say in church? "They have got a take-over spirit." No, it is not a take-over spirit; it is God. In some people it is an untamed act of dominion, but it is God. And so let's not criticize them; instead, let's bump you up, because right now you look like the servant. I want to show you how to get into the spirit-led life where you are manifesting exactly what God said that you could have, what God said that we could have, what God said that I could have.

To get to that point of thinking, there is a five-point plan to help. To take it, you have to change your thinking; you have to be more fruitful. Can you imagine the number of people who have lost their minds because they lost a job? Look at yourself and say, "Self, if you lost a job, you were looking for one when you found that one. So there is no need to lose your mind over that, or if you lost anything, there is no need to lose your mind because when you found that thing you were looking for it." So now people who understand that they are in charge don't get worried, they don't fizz out, they don't faint, they don't quit, they don't turn coward, and they don't get messed up when it is gone.

Understanding this mindset and this level of creativity means that the closer we move to God, the more we think like him, and this is not impossible.
Hebrews 9 says that the things that God will do for us are not based on how good we are. They are not going to result from works unless you have the opportunity to boast. According to what the Bible says, God's blessings are not going to be based on works even though we are not minimizing works. But they will require your work to keep them.

Mark 11, is where Jesus teaches the disciples about having faith. When we are living in this Spirit-led place beyond the veil, we will have started developing our relationship with God. In that particular place, you are saying that your will is not going to override what he says. In the first dimension, you had to distinguish your thoughts from thoughts that were projected to you. Not every thought was your thought. If you are going to walk this thing out by faith, you have to realize that not every thought was your thought even though it came into your head. Look at yourself and say, "Self, separate your thoughts." If we effectively separated our thoughts, we realize that not every thought that came into our head was our thought. We already understand that some of the thoughts were God's, and some of the thoughts were our own, but a great number of the thoughts in the first dimension were the Devil's thoughts. So now if we can separate the thoughts, then we get to move only on what God said or what is a thought approved by God. Not every thought is approved.

Have you ever allowed your mouth to fly open because you felt a symptom of something and called the symptom the thing? If I could have used my godly creative ability that I was born with when I saw the symptoms and then called for healing, then healing would have come.

Remember most of this happens at the level of your comprehension, right? If this happened at the level of your comprehension, then you need to make sure that you comprehend what God said. I can honestly say that we all heard this guy, Dr. Leroy Thompson. He came out with that, and he said that was a revelation that God gave him, and he said, "Now, this is not just a word. This is a prophetical word; the Lord gave me this word. Now, if you believe this is a prophetical word, and if you understand this and get the revelation on this, then you will never have another broke day in your life." And you know what? He said that month after month after month, year after year after year, but when it became revelation to me is when I actually tapped into it, and I never had another broke day. When I got the revelation of that man, do you know what? They didn't have to ask me to give I wanted to get that seed to him. I wanted to get that seed in the ground on that revelation. So that is what I did, and I never had another broke day in my life.

Now I don't know whether this makes sense to you, but most of you know that I have taken a 61 percent pay cut. But do you know what? I still haven't had a broke day. It still depends on whether or not you are fruitful because if you are fruitful, 61 percent only leaves space for opportunity to get it back and some. In Mark 11:22, Jesus tells the disciples, "Have faith in God." You would be well off if you could expect to never have another broke day in your life. If you can expect that, then that is what will happen to you. But now you have to work on the level of your expectation. It is a matter of development; in other words, what is the level of your development? Are you still developing yourself in a particular area, or did you stop? Where did your development stop? If you don't read every single day, somewhere along the line your development stopped. Every time we get to the point where we stop reading, we stop learning; we stop understanding, and our development stops.

Statistics say that those who in their lifetime have a consistent method of developing themselves through reading are the ones who are least likely to lose their minds. But the ones that don't develop themselves are more likely to lose their minds. Why is that? Your mind, just like your heart, is nothing but muscle, and if you don't exercise it, it goes back to flab. I am more disciplined mentally when I live a consistent life of exercising. The Lord told me that if you exercise, then every other area of your life where you are not completely disciplined will come into line. If you get into the habit of a regular, disciplined exercise program, then every other area of your life will come into alignment where you are not disciplined. And if you ever loosen up on that, the other areas start to come back because when you start putting pressure on yourself through exercise, you move into a whole different realm mentally where you are saying to every part of your life, "No, that is not healthy, and that is not going to be."

When I stop exercising, you can believe all those oatmeal, Oreo and Macadamia nut cookies, all of these other kinds of cookies, red velvet cake and cheesecake start coming back. My wife asks me if I want salad. No, I don't want any rabbit food. Why? I am comfortably setting back into the second dimension where no area of life can come into alignment without discipline in other areas. Choose an area of your life that you will work on to bring yourself into complete discipline.

It doesn't mean that you are going to be able to work on that area; sometimes we get to the place where we are chasing ghosts. What that means is that I am gaining weight, so I am going to stop eating cookies. But cookies are not the issue; they are ghosts. The Devil throws up all kinds of ghosts at me because I am looking at the surface of things. Instead of looking at the surface, I should be looking at the root of the thing. The root of the problem is that I don't exercise and lack discipline.

Twenty years ago I was drinking everything that I wanted to drink all the time. All of that ended with a decision. The greatest shout that I ever had was not in church—I had it in the liquor store because nobody thought that I would ever break drinking. My trunk was always full of drinks, and people were always accustomed to that, so no one believed that I would ever quit. I made a decision. Smoking two packs of cigarettes a day—guess what? All of it came with a decision. Every single thing that we have comes with a decision, but our mind has to become fruitful first. You will rise only to your level of comprehension. If you don't comprehend what God has made you, you will never rise to that point.

CHAPTER THREE

The Joseph Principle

God wants to do something very powerful in every one of our lives, and he is greatly depending on us to cooperate with him. Genesis 41 talks about Pharaoh's visions and Joseph's interpretations of those visions. We have been talking a lot about vision. We have been talking about our personal vision, and we have been talking about corporate vision. We have discussed financial management—putting some things into place in our lives to reach the position to accomplish God's work. In other words, the vision that God has predestined for us will be accomplished. I don't know about anybody else, but I want to go somewhere in God, and I am not satisfied being where I am and not advancing. I believe that God wants us to advance in the things of God. As a people, we need to prepare and plan to make sure we are advancing as a people. Too often we are almost directionless, having no goals, no dreams, no visions, and no aspirations. But way down inside, God is pulling something to tell us that we want something in life and that we aren't satisfied with where we are. We want to change our existence.

I don't know about anybody else, but that is me right there. I want to engage in activities that are going to change my existence, change what I look like financially, and change what I look like in every area of my life. I need to be going somewhere. You need to be going somewhere. God has given us powerful principles to apply to our lives to make things happen. Look at yourself and say, "Self, after this day I am going to make something happen." Nothing is going to happen just because we showed up, or just because we have a job. Nothing is going to happen just because God loves us. God loves us all, even the beggars that stand on the corner—you know God loves them.

But God's love for us is not going to change our situation. We have to actively get involved if our situation is going to change. I want to introduce you to the Joseph Principle. We have already talked about vision. Now we need to talk about provision. It is one thing to have a vision, but it is totally different to have provision. Without provision, the vision doesn't work.

Here's a very important question for you: Why should God give you the amount of money that you believe for? Are you believing for a greater amount of income? Why should God give that to you? In 2004 I was looking to double what I did in 2003, meaning not only financially but ministry-wise. The Devil had the audacity to show his tail off, so I am going to show my God off. If I am going to double the harvest, I have to get actively involved with God. Why should God give you the level of income or what you desire to accomplish in next year? If you are believing for an additional $100,000 this year, why should he do it? Is there anybody who would like to have another $100,000 next year? God can grant every last one of us an additional $100,000 next year, but why should he? What are we doing to justify that? God doesn't want you to have an additional $100,000 so it can just sit in the bank. It is a poor man's dream to have $100,000 to just sit in the bank. The bank will eat up the $100,000 that sat there while they pay you probably 1½ percent interest and 3 percent interest for having it in there. If I let you have $100,000 of my money to invest as you desire and get a great harvest from it, and then you are going to charge me 3 percent for loaning it, now who is the fool? There is nothing wrong with having money in the bank, but if you are going to have that kind of money, then we are going to need to make sure that we have a plan in place that is going to yield a greater harvest than 1 percent.

Why would God need to give you $100,000? How do you justify receiving that much from God? We already talked about vision, but with your vision comes God's provision. God wants to supply that to you, but he needs a reason. He doesn't want your reason to be buying a car that immediately loses value. But if we can justify God's provision, he will give it to us.

If God releases his provision to us, will we be bad stewards over it? What are you doing that requires $100,000 to make your vision happen? What is it that is written within your vision that says that you need $100,000? Do you have a vision? I am throwing some questions out there because you need to be able to answer in the event that God speaks to you today and tells you that he is ready to release $100,000 or $1,000,000 or another figure to you. You need to be able to instantly know exactly what you would do with that money. If you have to think about what you are going to do with it, then you are not ready for it. God wants to bring about provision, but he needs us to cooperate with him. He needs us to know what to do with his provision when it comes.

As we learn about provision, we have to understand that God, being a God of eternity and not a God of time, wants to give us something that is not necessarily meant for now. Here is the reality, and this may be a sad reality, but we are listening to God to hear what he is saying about now, and God is done talking to you about now. He already talked to you about now last year. So what he is talking to us about right now has to do with the next, coming year. Right now, God is looking ahead and working in the next year. So when we hear his Word regarding next year, we mistakenly think that God is talking about now. The provision that he wants to give you now is for next year.

God is going to start passing some stuff to you now, but you are going to have to be a good steward and realize that what he is getting ready to release to you right now is not meant for now. This means you can't increase your expenses as if God's provision is for now. God's provision regards our future, where we are going. Look at yourself and say, "Self, be sure and be double sure that you are a good steward, lest you starve next year." When we understand this, we won't know any days of lack. If we are in great need right now, the only reason is that we failed to pay attention last year. We were kicking up our heels last year, rejoicing about the abundance that came in. We purchased this and that and the other, not knowing that this year was coming. But now we are learning powerful principles that will enhance us where we are going. Look at yourself and say, "Self, our vision is at stake. Pay attention. I am going somewhere, How about you?"

If you came to hear a sad story, I don't have one to tell you. Instead, I have some good news: we are going somewhere. Stop complaining about the season you have been going through because it has been for one purpose only, to push you to where God wanted you to go. Whenever you need a push, God will create a season to make you dissatisfied with where you are. Please don't think that I am boasting; I am saying this only to prove a point. I came from driving only raggedy cars and living in places where you have to pray to go into the hood and pray to come out. When I was younger, if anybody was going to attack me, the best place to attack me was up front because I was always looking behind. That is the way I lived life. But now I am doing pretty well, driving better and living better than ever before. If I look at my current life based on where I came from, I can become satisfied with where I am. However, if I become satisfied with where I am, I will never reach forth to what God has for me.

I am by no means and you are by no means at the place that God wants us. You might be doing pretty well, but where you are right now is not at the level where God wants you. Until we become like one of his angels, we are not ever where he wants us.

God is sending provision right now for where we are going. Look at yourself and say, "Self, the vision is at stake." Once we learn that the vision is at stake, we need to walk according to the powerful principles to make sure that we don't waste God's provision in this season and cause the vision to fail. What do we need to do? Let's look at the Joseph Principle and at the powerful things in Genesis 41 that will help us get to where God wants us to go. God is telling us right now what we need to do to be in the correct position when it is time to fulfill the vision. Remember that Habakkuk says that the vision is yet for an appointed time. But when it is time for the vision to happen, provision is there because God starts in advance and doesn't wait until the time of fulfillment of the vision to prepare.

Joseph was a wonderful person. He reminds me about a lot of what God has spoken to us. Do you realize that when God first starts speaking to you about what he wanted you to accomplish in your life, you were by no means ready? Neither was I. Eighteen years ago God started dealing with me about my assignment, but I was not ready to do the assignment. I was not ready, but God was giving me information that I needed to prepare. If you badly want a word from the Lord, know that when God speaks to you, your seasons begin immediately. When God started dealing with me about where I was going, my season of preparation started immediately. I had to deal with some things. I had to deal with rejection. I had to deal with being talked about. I had to deal with having my name scandalized. I had to deal with hurt. I had to deal with heartache.

I had to deal with all of those things because when God got done with me, he needed to know whether or not I was going to be able to stand the test or turn coward and run. God wants to know that he can trust you to take the stand.

God starts talking to us early about things, and he started dealing with Joseph about a dream. But at first Joseph had a couple of issues. Number one, Joseph was immature. Number two, Joseph was arrogant. Joseph was by no means ready for the leadership that God told him that he would fulfill. When he started dreaming his dreams, he started boasting, "You know something, brothers? I am going to rule over you guys. I see you guys bowing down to me."(Now, if that happens to you, you don't have to talk about it as Joseph did.) But in spite of Joseph not being ready, God was speaking to Joseph in advance because he understood that Joseph was going to have to go through a season that was going to break down his arrogance. God has no problem with your being arrogant because he is not going to determine your destiny based on your level of arrogance right now. First, he will start a process to calm you down. So if you become too proud, God will calm you down because he is determined to get productivity from you. The season that we go through might be for the purpose of calming us down, or for some of us, the season might be for bringing us up. It depends on exactly where we are as individuals.

As we begin to deal with where we are going, we need to make sure that provision is happening in order to get us there. Joseph first had to endure specific seasons—a season of being forgotten about, a season of being rejected, a season of being sold into slavery, and other seasons for the different periods in his life. God used the seasons to prepare and position Joseph for the place of leadership in God's vision. Joseph's gift and skills positioned him in Pharaoh's house. Pharaoh summoned Joseph from the prison to interpret his dream. So Joseph prepared himself and interpreted Pharaoh's dream.

Pharaoh had a dream in which God showed Pharaoh a heathenish king exactly what was going to come—a famine. Why would God show the heathen what the future is going to be? God showed him because Pharaoh controlled the food and provisions in Egypt. God didn't give Pharaoh the dream because he was interested in Pharaoh eating, and God wasn't all that concerned about Egypt. God gave Pharaoh the dream because Pharaoh's provisions were going to be needed for God's people in Egypt under the covenant. Look at yourself and say, "Self, God will make sure that provision is made because he made you a promise."

God starts a process of putting provision in place because he is not going to watch us go down when he is giving us his Word. Every last one of us will have years of plenty, because the years of plenty do come. But our lack of management of God's provision during the season of plenty may cause us to end up in the midst of the vision having no provision left. We must brush up our management skills so that we are able to handle what comes after the years of plenty roll in when years of famine automatically follow. You will need to have provision or a surplus in place. That overflow will make sure that when those hard years come, they won't faze you.

Here is one of the things that we might mistakenly do. Let's say God has blessed us with another $10,000 to $20,000 raise on our job. The first thing that we do is spend more money and bump up our expenses. That is the wrong thing to do. This is your year of plenty, so don't bump up your expenses at this particular time.

Put the extra salary into the overflow to make sure that you have something stored up for the season of famine. In the years of plenty, we have to do what they did in Genesis 41:35, "And let them gather the food of those good years that come, and lay up corn under the hand of Pharaoh, and let them keep food in the cities." During these good years, Pharaoh had a dream about the cows and the good harvest and the fatted calf versus the ill favored calf and the ill favored harvest and all of that. Joseph interpreted the dream and told Pharaoh that seven years of plenty were coming, followed by seven years of famine. He advised Pharaoh how to store up food during the good years in order to be ready for the famine years. God wanted to make sure that the children of Israel would be fed during the famine years in Egypt.

Some of us wonder how the children of Israel ended up in Egypt. They went to Egypt because there was abundance there. See, you have to know when to go in and when to come out. The trick for me was that if I was going to gamble in my youth, I needed to know when to stop. I gambled and won so much that I wore my knees out, and I wasn't praying. All of the money was on my side, but I didn't know when to come back out. I convinced myself not to worry about the next time because the next time I might have absolutely nothing. You have to know when to go in and when to come out. This is another very powerful principle. I know that none of you are going to gamble. God has created a better way. We don't have to gamble now because we have guarantees of provision.

These years of plenty were extremely important years for the children of Israel because the vision was at stake. They went to Egypt, but they stayed too long. They stayed to the point where there was a new Pharaoh who did not know Joseph.

Just because they found grace with the first Pharaoh didn't mean they were going to find grace with the second. When you have years of plenty, God sets things up in order to make sure that the provision comes based on where he is taking you.

I am going to introduce you to the 70/30 principle now. This is the principle that I work by, but Joseph operated according to an 80/20 principle (the Joseph Principle). If you learn this, you will tap into days where there will be no lack. Joseph told the Pharaoh to store up 20 percent and have all of the people in the land live from the remaining 80 percent. I live according to a 70/30 principle. I spend 70 percent to live and save the remaining 30 percent. In other words, 10 percent for the tithe is automatic. My stuff will start to disappear out of my barn if I steal the 10 percent tithe. The 30 percent is divided into 10 percent for the tithe, 10 percent for short-term savings, and 10 percent for long-term savings.

So we need to create some kind of long-term savings that is going to be provision for us when we march into the vision. Watch out because temptation comes to get you to use some of your savings, especially the long-term 10 percent. It becomes tempting to use because you see that number constantly increasing. You see that number in your 401K or annuity accounts increase. When they told me how much I had in some of my insurance accounts, you know, I had to start speaking in tongues because it becomes a temptation when they tell you how much you can take out right now. You have to keep yourself in check so that you don't go to reaching for it because it is not for now. Look at yourself and say, "Self, it is not for now."

You have to keep telling yourself that because we like to buy things nowadays. We are like the wasteful prodigal son who asked his father to give him his inheritance and then wasted all of it.

There is a principle that goes into motion when you use up all of your stuff: nobody gives anything else to you. Nobody gave anything to the prodigal son. How can you be in a position like that, where no one gives to you? Ask any beggar on the street. Thousands of us pass them by and don't give them a dime. Do you know why? There is nothing that they possess that puts a demand on our money.

When you show up with a vision, there is a demand that is put on people's money. Saved or unsaved, there is a demand that is put on their money—not put on them. God has arranged all of this. Here is what you and I are. If we are tithers and we have a vision, then we become money magnets. There is a demand that is placed on other people's money because we have a vision, so you have to make sure you have a vision. Somebody is looking for you, and they want to give to you. They even want to invest in what you are doing, but they have to know you have a vision. How many of you are going somewhere?

Choose either the 80/20 principle or the 70/30 principle. Do you realize next year I ought not to be living off a 70/30 principle? If I obey God, I should be living off a 60/40 principle. God starts to get interested in me because he sees that I am now bumping up my income—I didn't say my salary—I am bumping up my income and decreasing some expenses for stuff that I really don't need. Fast food is going to work right through me, so I don't need to spend and still be hungry by the time I leave work.

Next I want to talk about Pharaoh's management team. Anybody who doesn't have a management team in place is set up for a fall, and anybody who ignores that management team is set up for a fall.

In leadership class, we talk about church leadership, church government, political government, and family government. If any one of these groups ignores the system, the vision cannot be completed. Even a family ought to have a vision. For my family, I am believing for my children to be millionaires, and I am believing for my children's children to be set. This means that I will have to put some principles in place if it is going to happen in my generation so I can hand it down to their generation. So there is a team that needs to be put in place.

Look at Genesis 41:33-34. Pharaoh is recognized as the president, the absolute head, and now he brings Joseph, the administrator or the governor, on the scene and says to Joseph, "The only place you are not as great as I is the throne, and I give you authority over all of my stuff." Who has authority over all of your stuff? Or are you so scared or are you so controlling that you don't want anybody to have that level of authority to tell you what you can and can't spend? Come on, somebody has to call those kinds of shots. There are times that I get a call from my niece early in the morning to tell me to stop spending, don't write any more checks, don't do this, don't do that. Because I am the president and I have already laid down the rules, when she calls me and says no more spending, I have to submit to that or I overthrow the vision. The vision is what I would overthrow, so I would hurt my kids and myself because overspending sets me back on my plan.

We have also set up the finance officers. One of my finance officers, my daughter, is the like the governor. She assists me at home as one of my finance officers. She makes sure that I have my receipts and everything in order. I have to do my part, so I jot down my spending and write receipts so we won't have any trouble when it is time to write off some stuff. We have a backup system. So I have to submit to my daughter.

I brought her in the earth? So what, I submit to her because she is one of the finance officers and is taking care of my finances as a team with my niece. My son, Junior, needs to understand my need to submit to them. He needs to hope that I submit to the other two, or when he has a need, it is over. But with a good management team, stopping spending doesn't mean we're broke; it just means that according to the budget I have to stop spending awhile. When you have your management team set up right, it doesn't mean you are broke. I will never have another broke day in my life as long as I think ahead. Don't think after you become broke. Start thinking now. The vision comes from the president, the governor is the one who is governing the stuff, and the finance officers have their responsibilities. We have a vision for our family. We are going somewhere.

The finance officers have different responsibilities, such as gathering, as in Genesis 41:35, where we read the words, "gather," "lay up," and "keep." When I think about this passage, I see that Joseph had his stuff together, and he didn't learn this stuff at home. Joseph learned from the seasons he went through. When Joseph was in the pit, no one was throwing any food down there to him, so he had to ration whatever was put down there and properly manage the stuff. When he ended up in slavery, nobody was going to over feed him, so whatever came along, he had to manage. So what he taught Pharaoh was what he had learned from the seasons that he was in. He didn't learn this at home, and most of us who come from dysfunctional families didn't learn it at home either.

I learned some of this stuff because I had to. My dad used to get paid every week, so I didn't learn how to make a salary last longer than that when I was growing up. But when I had a job myself, I was paid monthly and had to learn how to stretch out that paycheck for a whole month.

I was raising five children by myself. My children didn't always like my little management skills when I was making little or nothing. But you know what? When I got paid, dinner was not going to be fast food. It was a red tag day when I took them for fast food. You know what? Grocery store, here we come. I hope you have that buy-one-get-one-free deal today, because here we come. Now we weren't going to do it in grand style, but we did porkettes because we couldn't afford the pork chops. The children almost dreaded carrying the bags into the house because they knew they were full of porkettes. Sometimes we could do some level of celebrating, meaning that I was cooking meatloaf. A red tag day was my cooking cabbage, macaroni and cheese, or maybe rice and meatloaf. But this was not going to be every day. We couldn't afford that because we were going somewhere. I had to remain conscious of that, and so if we were going somewhere, we couldn't afford pork chops and meatloaf every day. We were not going to do it.

Please don't ask my children the last time they had a porkette. They don't remember because we are not there anymore. We are not doing steak every day now, but management skills have to be in place or you will overthrow what God is trying to provide for you. Because God is more conscious of the vision than you are, he starts to send the stuff when he understands that you have the vision in mind. When God sends you an extra hundred dollars, remember that God has the vision in mind. This is part of the overflow that is stored in the various cities of Egypt.

You need the right variety of people on your management team to handle your finances. You cannot send the guard to gather the stuff. We can't expect the tightwad, who keeps the money, to gather it. And you need the tightwad or you will spend everything.

Your gatherers know how to make money by coming up with ideas to bring in resources, but a gatherer is not designed to lay it up or store it. You also need somebody who knows how to take what you have made and to be the carrier of that and store it in the bank. If you have a spender try to do the storing, they might spend the money before it gets to the bank. Your whole system would be in trouble, and your vision would be in trouble. I want a dependable person to make my deposits. Then you need those who know how to guard it. When the cities of Egypt stored the food, somebody needed to understand how to guard it.

We have to go back to the three governmental systems—political government, church government, and family government. If the family is really going to make it, we need a tightwad person in place. I can't begin to tell you how important that position is because without the tightwad we will end up spending everything. Most gatherers have a retail kind of a mindset, knowing how to use ideas to bring resources in. But if we don't have somebody to guard the storehouse, then we are in trouble. I need to be able to submit to that and agree to do without things that are not in the budget. If the family does not understand how to submit to this kind of process, then the vision is overthrown. What is at stake in overthrowing the vision? Maybe God will stop sending his provision because you don't have a governing system and budget in place. And then you have to know where you stand as you make different decisions.

We have to consider the characteristics of this management team. If all of the characteristics are not in place, you can't handle the money because the vision is at stake. Look at yourself and say, "Self the vision is at stake."
So the characteristics that are involved say whether or not you will be able to handle your money. Let me give you the characteristics: you have to be discrete, be wise, and have the spirit of God.

We talked about this in a leadership class. How do you know when to give? Are you giving to the poor, or are you giving to the beggar? If you give to the beggar, you have no reward. You have nothing coming back—nothing, nothing, nothing. If you give to the poor, the Bible says he that give to the poor lends to the Lord and the Lord shall repay him again. If I am properly governing my stuff, then what that says is that when I help somebody, if I am giving to the poor, don't look for a harvest. I am not giving to the poor to get a harvest, and I have to understand that. If you are giving to the poor, you are not really looking to get a harvest because that is not how you get a harvest. He that gives to the poor lends to the Lord and the Lord shall repay him again—in other words, you are going to get what you put in. If you gave him a dollar, you are going to get a dollar back because the Lord is only repaying you.

This must be understood if I give to a beggar. A beggar is somebody who shows up before you get to your stop at 7:00 in the morning to make sure that he has the right cup and the right spot to make sure that he catches you as you are going by to go to work. In contrast, the poor are trying to do something for themselves. The bottom line is this: God is going to judge me on what I did with my money, and he is going to judge whether or not I stand as a faithful steward based on what I did with my money. So just because somebody walks up to my car with a cup out doesn't mean that I am going to put anything in it. You know what, I am not cheap by a long shot. As a matter of fact, I am a giver by nature. Stuff doesn't matter to me because if I treat all of my stuff as if it is God's, then God will treat all of His stuff as if it is mine.

I have to be a good steward over the stuff. I said all of that to say that they have to be discrete, they have to be wise, and they have to have the spirit of God in them. And now I can trust them with my stuff because they have the wise spirit of God in them.

When we have those powerful principles in place, there is nothing that God will withhold from us, not one single thing. God will not withhold anything from us because we execute powerful principles. We understand what to do, when to do it, and how to do it. We already understand this. We start right where we are because the provision comes in for one reason: to be a supply for the vision. We have a vision for our personal lives, we have a corporate vision that is a vision for the church, and we have a vision for businesses that we put into place, and, therefore, God wants to provide or bring about provision for those visions.

CHAPTER FOUR

Prosperously Prepared By a Season

Genesis 37 describes the dreams that Joseph had showing the vision for his life. We have been talking about having a personal vision for our lives, including how to use the Joseph Principle. I believe that we are in a moment right now where we will be able to embrace what God is doing and wants to do in our lives, and we need to be able to handle whatever it is that God releases to us. We need to be able to effectively and properly manage what he gives us. God wants us to be able to manage what he puts into our hands, and as we do that well, we will find that more will show up. God rewards those who are faithful over a few things. If you can be faithful over a few things, God will reward you with more. Does that make sense to you?

This is important. Do you realize that most of us do not have financial problems? We have financial management problems because we have not been effectively managing what came in, then we think that we have a financial problem. Then we think that we need another job, and we think that we need a part-time job, and before you know it we have two full-time jobs, two part-time jobs, and ends are still not met. As a result, do we sacrifice worship in order to meet a natural need? Are we sacrificing the time that we are supposed to have with God so that we can meet a natural need? Something is wrong with that picture. It is because we have not effectively managed what we have, and because we have not effectively managed it, now all of a sudden we mentally think we have a financial problem.

If I could turn on my radar and look into your checkbook, I would be able to tell you if you have a financial management problem. Look.

The three checks you forgot to put in your register may cause you to bounce some, and now some money that you did not plan to go out now went out in a $35 bank charge for bouncing the checks. And then on the other side, where the check was written to, they want to slap you with a charge, too, because you should have known what was in the account. When we manage our money properly and wisely, God will cause more to show up. Let's come up to today. We need to talk about these things so we can move into a place where we can have what we need. Look at yourself and say, "Self, God wants you to have exactly what you need and what you desire, that is the Word of the Lord as it concerns you." God wants you to have that, but he can't allow us to have it if we are not managing properly.

Let's say for instance you are married. If both people have jobs, yet they are still operating as two single people, you are bad managers. The two strings should have come together. Now I realize that there are some circumstances where you can't do that because one person's spending is out of control and they won't submit, and that is not an anti-female statement. When it comes down to the operation of the house, both parties have to submit and come together to calculate all of the bills of the house. I realize that here is where we have one of the problems. You know most women earn more money than the man does. That is correct in most cases, not all cases, but it is correct in most cases. Let's say for instance she is earning $60,000 a year, and he is doing $20,000 a year. The income of the household is $80,000. You wouldn't have $80,000 without the $20,000, so it is not constructive to say that you make more and I make less. When you are putting it all in the same pot, it is the same. When somebody asks you the question your annual income, $80,000 is the answer. You two are longer two different individuals but are one, and the income is the total regardless of who caused it to come.

But when we don't effectively manage that income, we have real problems. Because if we have somebody on the team who doesn't manage the money properly, won't submit, and spends every dime, then for the well-being of the house we may have to have separate accounts. Why? That person is going to spend everything. That person is going to bounce checks and not tell you about it. You won't know that a check has bounced until you are the one who shows up at the mailbox first. The other person will rush to the mailbox because the bank is going to send a notice. We may need separate accounts in a case like that so we will not be out on the street. My daddy told me if nothing else gets paid, the rent or mortgage gets paid. The whole system is going to go down if we have one rebel on the team, especially if the rebel has access to the money.

You need to know how to get money into the bank, into your hands, so that you will know how to attract what is supposed to come. We have to know how to attract it. Here is a powerful principle that I heard a man of God teach. He said that the thing that you disrespect will get away from you, so if you disrespect money it will get away from you, and the things that you respect will be attracted to you, meaning they will hunt you down and find you. If you disrespect money, it will run away from you. It will stay from you in a big way. You will live from paycheck to paycheck because you disrespect money. Look at yourself and say, "Self, you are going somewhere, and God is going to help you to get there."

In this season of our lives, God is going to break bondages that we have held onto. Your bondages really don't bother God, and God is about to break the bondages in this second wind that he is getting ready to give us. We all have sin, and then there are bondages that are least likely to be identified as bondages. I don't think we need to talk about sin every Sunday. If you know you have sinned, admit it, get rid of it, all of that.

But I want to talk about bondages that God has dealt with me about that most of us don't realize are bondages. One bondage is the lack of finances. Even though that is a bondage, we won't treat it as a bondage.

Here is the thing about God. God will allow you to walk around with nothing if that is what you want. God will allow you to have nothing if you don't rise up. Look at yourself and say, "Self, you have to get desire inside you in order to come out of that bondage of lack of finances." If you want an old clunker, God will let you have it, but that is not where you should park. If you want to live in an old shack, God will let you, but that is not where you should park—in other words, don't stop there. It is a process to get up, and I understand that. I'm not coming against that, I'm not coming against the clunker because the clunker is designed to get you to the next vehicle, and there's nothing wrong with that. When it comes down to financial bondage, God will let you stay there if that is what you want to do. He is not going to twist your arm.

Many of us expect God to smack us up out of poverty, but God says we must desire to leave poverty and lack of material goods. God will let you stay there. It is a bondage, and a lot of us operate right there. Some of us have become comfortable with a particular level of living. Some people have lived smack dab in the ghetto. I was only one hood over from the ghetto. You could stand in the middle of the ghetto and throw a rock to where I lived. I was close. Where I lived we were the outcast because we weren't bad enough to really be associated or carry the name Kenilworth, the street I lived on. On the other side of us were the wonderful houses, and we weren't doing well enough for them to accept us. They called us "the creek boys" because we had a creek on the back side of our house. We had to decide that is not how we wanted to exist for the rest of our lives. There was a wonderful woman (I don't know if she was a woman of God) over in Kenilworth who decided that she didn't want Kenilworth to continue to look the way it appeared. Decisions had to be made so that we could experience something better, but guess what? As long as Kenilworth was like that, God just let it be. He didn't like it, but he let it be just like that. And you know what? You can decide today how you want to live, and then God will get involved because you have effectively become a dreamer.

You have to dream about better things. My sister is a great example. She doesn't know it, but we used to make fun of her because we didn't understand her. She was a little "off," or at least we thought she was because she would just wake up one morning and decide, "I want a new living room set." Her decision wasn't messed up, but we thought it was odd that when she made that decision she would give away her old stuff, even if there wasn't anything wrong with it, and she didn't even wait until the new stuff came. She didn't have a dime to put towards the new stuff, so we thought she was crazy. We'd visit her house and find an empty living room and wonder what was up. She would say, "Oh, I'm getting a new living room set," and within one week it would be there. Where did the money come from? When you have a dream, money will show up. When you have dreams and make a move of faith, money shows up.

My sister taught us something. She talked about her vision as if the furniture was already on the delivery truck. She was operating in the faith of God, and she wasn't even saved. The God kind of faith will work for anybody who applies the principle. You don't have to be saved. This is the reason that the Lord said, "I speak in parables so that they seeing might not see and hearing they might not hear lest in their present heart condition they be converted and should heal them." What God is literally saying is that I am literally bound by my word. Even if I am unsaved, I am bound by my word. I can't say that I can't do this for this person who is unsaved and have them believe me.

When we have a dream, we tap into principles that make the dream work. Why would Joseph share his dream with his brothers if he expected his enemies to hinder his dream? He shared his dream because the power of a dream is stronger than any enemy in the earth. They tried to kill Joseph, but he refused to die because of his dream. Joseph had to be made accountable, so he spoke his dream. If you don't speak your dream, who is going to keep you accountable? When the going gets tough, if I have hidden my dream, if I have internalized my dream, then I don't have as much incentive to succeed when the going gets tough. So I talk about my dream, especially to haters, because now I need an incentive to not to give up on my dream. So tell your haters about your dream. When you tell your haters your dream, your haters are going to talk about you like a dog if you don't bring it to pass. When the going got tough for Joseph, he thought, "I'm not going to die in the pit, I'm not going to die in slavery; I'm not going to die in any of those other places where they sold me." Your haters will not let you live it down if you don't make it. You will have an incentive to fulfill your dream so you are not talked about as a failure. Look at yourself and say, "Self tell your most important dream to a hater."

Next is your occupational progress or lack of occupational progress. God wants you to progress. Here is the question: Are you marketable? Are you employed somewhere? What would make them pass out a pink slip to everybody but you? Let's kill the myth they are not going to lay you off because you are the highest paid and because they understand you are too valuable to the company's future. Making the most money won't save your job, so let's kill that myth right now. What is it that you bring to the company that nobody else in the company can do? Are you marketable?

I am not against low positions in a company because all positions are valuable. But if you are a broom pusher, any person with muscles can do that, so you are more expendable. If you take too many days off, you are out of here because we can get another broom pusher. If you are in the data entry field, unless you are pumping out 120 words per minute, you might be replaceable. I haven't heard of anybody who can type 120 words per minute, but I guess it is possible. If you type 50 words per minute, we can get anybody to do that except for me, but I am working on it.

How are you going to make yourself marketable? Two of our downfalls are unwillingness to learn and fear of change. Most of us are afraid of really making ourselves marketable. Don't stay in a dead-end job just because you have been on this job for ten years. God wants you to progress and start from where you are.

We have competition in our occupations. For example, there are many versions of Schools of the Prophets being created. But I am not intimidated because I haven't seen anybody else who can do what I do with the school. Anybody can teach the School of the Prophets, but what God told me to do specific things that nobody else is doing. You, too, have a specific purpose from God. Let's say, for instance, that you are a teacher. Any trained person can teach, but what makes you stand out as different? What kinds of results are you having with those kids or with your group?

How do you stand out as different? What makes you more marketable than the next person? Anybody can wash a car, but what makes you stand out? Is it the way you put that shine on that car? If you have a company, what makes your company different that would make folks step over a thousand other companies in order to get to yours? Do we understand why people will step over any other church to get to ours, or any other church to get to yours?

Stop trying to be a cheap carbon copy of somebody else. We have to be marketable. You need this information right now and for many days to come. God is saying that a financial shift and an occupational shift are coming. All kinds of companies are going to go through a shift. They are going to have to pull out the most marketable people and set them up as the ones that will train the new group that they are bringing in. Will you be on the pink slip crew, or are you going to be on the crew that is going to start right now making yourself marketable? Look at yourself and say, "Self, I'm going to work on you to make sure that I am more marketable than anybody else I know."

It requires me to work on myself and become dissatisfied with where I am. We cannot think until we make it because they are going to look at our work progress and examine us according to that. So stop complaining about doing the job of ten people. Just do the job because it all boils down to reaching your dream. I have a dream to be president of this company. That is what it boils down to: I have a dream. I am not just passing by; I have a dream. And I'm not just talking about having a dream. I dream about being rich—absolutely, holy rich. Why do riches have to be filthy? I have a dream, not so I can get the biggest house or drive the biggest car.

It might be nice to have a limousine, but it would probably get lonely back there in a limousine by myself, far away from the driver. I have a dream. You have a dream. Pursue your dream.

I want to be rich to finance the work of God in the earth. If my pastor calls me and says he wants to go on television, I want to make the transfer for his first year on television. I don't want to have to examine the budget first; I want to be able to just write the check. You have to dream of being the one who is able to write the check. Do you know what? When I write the first few million-dollar checks, I'm going to remind you that I came from right next door to the ghetto so I can fulfill my purpose of reaching my dream based on where I came from. I need to remind you about where I came from to inspire you about God's power for your dreams. I know preachers who have come from the ghetto, preachers who used to sell drugs but flying around in jets now, not with drug money. They bought the stuff and got there by dreaming. I want to see if we can get your dreams molded, shaped, fashioned into godly dreams so that we can go to a level in God where he desires us to be. Look at yourself and say, "Self, we are going somewhere." Start dreaming about it. When you see somewhere that you want to go, get something to remind yourself about where you are headed.

Let's briefly review what we have been talking about. We talked about the Joseph Principle. We said it's imperative to pay attention to the seasons of our

lives. We said we should extract the negatives and positives, and especially magnify the positives so we don't cheat ourselves from getting what God wants us to experience in each season. Sometimes we don't see the positives because we magnify the negatives too much. Regardless of what has ever happened in our lives, we can take every season and get something out of that season.
It doesn't matter what the season was, it doesn't matter what happened, it doesn't matter whose fault it was. We can extract the positive, see the negative for what it is, and go over the top of where we have supposed to have been going.

As we begin to deal with particular things, we will see that there is an Enemy that has been released to cancel out every single thing that we have been designed to bring to pass in order to stop God in what he wanted to bring in the earth. It is very important that we see every single thing in our season that God wants us to see and bring to pass what he intends for us to bring to pass.

We need to think about bringing provision into our lives. We talked about Pharaoh and the management team that he set up in order to bring to pass and properly manage what God had put into place. We talked about the gatherer, the storer, and the guard. We talked about them in terms of management teams in the family, church, business, and our personal lives. We need to set up a team around ourselves in order to accomplish every single thing that God has predestined that we accomplish in our day. Look at yourself and say, "Self, you need a team to cause everything to happen that God wants to happen in your life." We will never accomplish anything great by ourselves. We will never get it done without a team. That is one of the reasons that people who exist by themselves never really do anything great. We talked about the submission that we should have to those who gather, lay up, and store and guard, and how important our submission is to our success.

There is a reason why you exist, and until we really tap into the "why," the "what" never happens. If we can understand why we exist, then we will move into a greater dimension and a greater ability to make things really happen in our lives. We might be tired of going through seasons and not understanding why we had to go through them. But we must understand that God allowed the season to happen. Even if a season happened because we caused it or the Devil caused it, God allowed it to happen. I didn't even say that God permitted it to happen; there is a difference between what he allows and what he permits. But now that we are in this particular season, let's make the best out of it in order to bring the fullness of what God intended to come to pass. Let's learn to extract the positives from it. Let's go ahead and enjoy working this thing out. If you are dealing with a challenge right now go ahead and enjoy the pleasure of working this thing out and seeing it through.

I need to share with you two experiences during one season in my life. I thought that I had a reason to quit, but I had a "why" inside me that wouldn't let me quit. This was when I was launched into the position of raising my five children by myself. The other experience was when I was disabled. These two experiences happened almost simultaneously. A year after God spoke to me and called me into ministry; I became disabled and was in the position raising the five children by myself. In my mind the Devil hollered, "God must have made a mistake. There is no way that God called you. Look at your situation." We have come to a point where we have judged what we are called to do by what we are going through now.

This is the way the Devil talks us out of what God has called us to do. We look at where we are, not at what is going on in our lives right now, and then judge, "God could not have possibly told me that. Rodney, you must have missed it big time because look at what's going on right now. You are disabled. You say that God called you to preach the Gospel, called you to preach faith into the life of his people.

He has called you to do this, he has called you to pastor, and he has called you to do all of these things, and look at your life, Rodney." This is what the Devil was hollering at me, and I was helping him. He was telling me that my life was a mess and that I was not qualified to preach faith because I was disabled.

God was speaking a Word to me at this particular time. But the Devil said, "Now, look. You are raising five children by yourself. How are you going to preach the Gospel? When are you going to have time to study? What are you going to do? How are you going to do this, Rodney?" The "how" is none of your business. If you know your reason, then don't worry about the how. We get stuck worrying about how, but the answer comes with the process of time. We become too engrossed in the how, which is futuristic. We can't deal with now. If I understand my reason "why," the "how" will show up automatically.

How? Let's look at this in light of what God said regarding Joseph. Every season prepares you for where you are going, for "why" you exist. But its effectiveness will be according to how you view what you have gone through. Do you view this season as something that is designed to kill you (and, yes, it is designed to kill you)? Do you view this season as something that has been designed to destroy you? Yes, it is designed to destroy you, but that is not what your focus ought to be. Your focus ought to be on using the season to connect with the people whom you need to meet and the vehicle that you need to stand on to get to the next level. This is the reason this season showed up in my life.

This is very important. As we look at Joseph's situation, we can better understand why he went through it, and you, too, will come to understand why you go through different seasons.
God sent Joseph, and as we read in Genesis 45:5, God sent him to preserve life. The reason you and I have experienced seasons is that there is an assignment on our lives to preserve life. Your seasons lead you to a point in your life when you cause somebody else to live. Until we really understand this, we won't extract everything that we need to extract from our seasons and testing periods. Something exists inside you that gives you a reason not to quit.

When I was going through my particular season, I talked about two experiences, yet both were during one season. When I went through that season, I came to understand that I should not count it as bad. I should not count it as something that the Devil wanted to use in order to kill me and count me out. We have to learn to cause that to be a level of octane that will now motivate us and empower us for this next level.

Look at yourself and say, "Self, the season that I have just gone through is going to serve as octane. It is going to serve as petrol to motivate me and empower me on this next level." It is going to serve as what I need on this next level to motivate me, to empower me, and to give me the next push that I need. Because when I look back, I am going to get a benefit by my looking back at what I have gone through. I will realize that my rocket power is behind me.

Understand this: God sent Joseph to preserve life. Once he understood his purpose, this gave him reason to keep existing even though he was in prison, even though he was sold into slavery, even though he went down into all of those deep pits. His purpose, his "why," gave him a reason to keep on living because while he was down in the pit he understood his "why," and when he was sold into slavery he understood his "why," and so his "why" was greater than his need to quit. When I was going through my season, my "why" had to be greater than my reason to quit.

Let me ask you this: What you have gone through in your life? Every last one of us has felt like quitting something, right? Whether or not you really had a reason to quit, was your "why" greater than your reason to quit? My "why" says that God sent me to preserve life. I cannot die in the pit because my "why" says that I must exist to bring life to somebody else. Regardless of failures, regardless of your difficulties, regardless of the season that tried to count you out that tried to kill you, regardless of the Enemy that doesn't agree with what you are doing and why you are doing it, regardless of any of that, my "why I exist" has overridden my reason to quit.

I could have done one of two things in my life. I could have quit, but my "why" was greater than my reason to quit. I want to talk to you about your "why you exist." My "why I existed" was to preserve life. My children weren't going to happen if I did not develop a "why I exist." I could have cried while I was braiding their hair and just allowed it to end with a tear, and, yes, there were many days that I cried while I was braiding hair because I didn't know what I was doing. But I concentrated on what I was doing based on my "why."

Just as I have been called to preserve life, what God has placed inside you calls you to preserve life for somebody else. It is not about you and what you are going through. Stop listening to your emotions because your "why" is too important. Let's look at Genesis 45:5, "Now therefore be not grieved, nor angry with yourselves, that ye sold me hither: for God did send me before you to preserve life."
After what Joseph went through, isn't it amazing that he could say to his brothers, "God sent me ahead of you in order to preserve you"? The Bible does not say that Joseph totally ignored everything that his brothers did and absolutely forgave them. He says, "I am not charging this to you because God sent me. I understand the why I was in that position. God sent me ahead to preserve life for you."

One of my daughters told me just the other day that she was glad she was able to stay with me, because if she hadn't, she wouldn't have been doing as well as she is today. Who you are with will determine what you will become. A great man of God I was listening to said this, "Your network will determine your net worth." In other words, if you consider everybody that you are hanging around with right now, if you know more than they know, you are in bad shape. In order to work on your vision, you need to have people around you who are greater than you and not be intimidated by their greatness but be motivated by their greatness. When we hook up with people, we need to evaluate how they are greater than we are. If you cannot see how they are greater than you are, you are wasting your time.

Joseph did this. He understood that God had to send him ahead of his brothers because although he had the dream around them, standing around them with the dream would not have enabled him to fulfill it. He had to leave his brothers in order to produce what was designed to preserve them. The guys on the corner have wonderful dreams, but their dreams stay on the corner. They dream about having houses and cars and a wonderful wife, and I can imagine women dream of having a wonderful husband and having something out of life. But we have to decide to get up off the corner and find somebody who is greater to assist us. Until we do that, nothing will happen.

One of the reasons that I love being at church on Sundays is that I feel the energy of every member of the congregation. You are in church because God has deposited something inside you to make something happen in church. When you leave church, you ought to be so ignited with what God has said to you that you ought to go out there on a Sunday evening or on a Monday morning and have people look at you and say you look dangerous because you appear ready to make something happen.

My reason for existing has to be greater than my reason to quit. God sent Joseph to bring salvation by great deliverance. One reason that troubled people seem to come around you is that they realize that something exists inside you, and if they can get close enough to have contact with you, then they will have what they need to make the next thing happen in their lives. Look at yourself and say, "Self, you will never get it done by yourself". Joseph was to save by great deliverance. Look at this in the Word. God spoke a Word to you in Genesis 45:7, "And God sent me before you to preserve you." He said, "I am not mad at you. Don't be mad at yourselves, because I know my 'why.'" This can help us to forgive anybody who has done anything to us, no matter what the person did. Understanding your "why" will keep us in the level of the love of God. Some people will never, ever leave where they are unless a major catastrophe happens. We will always sit on that seat of offense if something doesn't happen. This is the reason you can forgive anybody. Why can't you forgive somebody? The reason is that you don't understand your "why," and you want to blame them for your not understanding your "why."

I am going to exist either in my "why" or in my reason. Some folks quit their job, but they go there every morning.
They quit a long time ago, but they keep on going there because they don't understand their "why," and so they are living in their reason. But if the season that I have on this job is only to prepare me for where I am going, do you know what? I am going to do the best job that I can do in this season because there may be a contact that will be made in this job that will launch me to the next place.

Stop getting mad at folks and blaming folks because you don't understand your "why." I am not mad at anybody. If you are really not mad at them, then you will have no problem being around them. However, I won't be around them if they aren't part of my "why," because they will keep launching me into my reason to quit.

Let me give you something real that happened to me in my season. There were some people I had to get away from, people who suggested that I separate my children among different relatives, sisters, aunts, and grandparents to divide up the child care.

But the children became my "why I had to exist"; without my "why I had to exist" I would have died. One reason that people die is that they lose their "why."

My father, now that he has retired, refuses to go back south. He says that because everybody that he knows that retires and goes back south dies. If that is at all true, here is the reason: when they go back south in retirement, they lose their "why." If I had separated my children, I would have disconnected the parts of my "why," and my "why" would not have existed. I would have absolutely been left open for the Devil to make me do anything that he wanted me to do. I would have ended up in a position where whatever goes until I died. I would have died at that point of losing my "why."

Joseph says that all of this was intact, all of the brothers, mom, and dad—that was intact—and that God had sent him ahead of the rest of the family. They were not disconnected, but Joseph had to go ahead of you and go through everything that he needed to go through because they were his "why." Look at yourself and say, "Self, you are my 'why I exist;' I exist to preserve life for you. So I can never become disconnected from my 'why.' "While Joseph was in prison he painted pictures on the wall of his "why," his brothers and his mother and his father and all of them back home, so he could never lose sight of his reason he was going through his seasons. Once you lose sight of your "why", once you lose sight of your goals, once you lose sight of all of that, you literally die. Have a wonderful understanding of your "why." You are preserving life for somebody because God wants to set some of us in charge.

God indeed is going to do a transfer of the wealth of the wicked into the hands of the just, and it is going to be because the just got into the position where the wicked are. God has not changed. When I understand my "why," then I will quit trying to get positioned with all of those that are familiar to me in places that I am familiar with. When God wanted to preserve the nation of Israel at one point, he had Mordecai, who was the mentor and the uncle of Esther, get Esther into a heathenish beauty pageant. You may not think this was appropriate behavior, but when God understands your "why," you will be found in some of the weirdest situations. You know that Christians are not supposed to take part in beauty pageants, at least according to the old school of thinking, because you have to put on makeup and perfumes and heathenish garments and all of this.

Mordecai showed Esther how to get ready. How in the world could a man prepare a woman for a beauty pageant? There was a process to follow for entering this beauty pageant. A Jewish girl entering a heathenish beauty pageant soaked herself in perfume so when the king was ready to make another selection, she smelled wonderful, looked good, and was attractive. She and her head were all covered. Because God wanted to do a major transfer, he had to get her in the beauty pageant and she had to be attractive to this heathenish king. So it meant that her name and clothes had to be changed.

Now not only did God send Esther into that kind of situation, sending a Jewish girl to a heathenish king, but he also sent Joseph into that kind of situation, sending a Jewish boy to serve a heathenish king. What Esther and Joseph also had in common was that they were to preserve their nation—their "why." We too, have to make sure that we correctly carry what God wants us to carry for this generation. As Genesis 45:7-8 show God's vision for Joseph, in the same way God is preparing you.

If you don't write down your goals, you are not going to accomplish anything great. When we come to church, we shouldn't just look at it as a Sunday morning message. We have effectively become unreligious, so we won't have any religious Sunday morning service or religious conferences. We won't have any more of that. If it doesn't add something to you, let's not do it. You can just go ahead and throw on some real good music going down the road if you just want to shout. I have this stereo in my car, and sometimes if I want a good shout I just crank up a Mark Livingston CD going down the road. Thank God I have "Pastor" written on the back of my car, because the only thing you can hear is the bass, but it is gospel.

When I come to church, I want some Word to talk to me about ideas and dreams that are going to happen the next five years of my life so I can use the Word and see that yes, this has happened, and that has happened, and the other has happened. Glory be to God, I am on my way in Jesus. Every now and then I have to snap the religious circle and the religion out so you will know where we are, because for too long we have been too religious, and Sunday morning has only been a little tea party. It can't be a tea party anymore. It has to be a major time where we come together for brainstorming and coming together with ideas and visions and dreams, sharpening them so that when we get out there on a Monday morning we know we are going somewhere. When I step foot on my job, I have to know that something around here is getting ready to change.

God sent me three words that stood out to me as I read this passage of Genesis, and I am going to say this to you prophetically. A transfer is going to happen for the saints. If you are saved, this is going to happen for you, and God is going to set up the time where this is going to happen. I am saying this to every last one of you prophetically. These are the three words: father, lord, and ruler. Genesis 45:7-8 reads, "And God sent me before you to preserve you a posterity in the earth, and to save your lives by a great deliverance. So now it was not you that sent me hither, but God: and he hath made me a father to Pharaoh, and lord of all his house, and a ruler throughout all the land of Egypt."

Father, lord, ruler here is how the transfer happens. As we go along, God tells us about how he made Joseph a father to Pharaoh. Joseph affected Pharaoh's life in such a way that Pharaoh listened to everything that Joseph said. God will give you the hookup and a position with whoever is head over all of where you are. You really have to get this.

God will give you position with that person, be it male or female. God will give you position with that person, and they will listen to everything that you say. You can't say "lord." You have to say "lord over his entire house" so that everybody under his charge starts to listen to you because of the favor that you have with him.

God starts to set you up and give you position. I want you to lock this in. When you look over the next year, I want you to just think about this Word right here. Some of you are going to find that this is going to start happening, if it hasn't already happened. God is not going to hook you up with the Vice President. He is going to hook you up with the chief person, and you will find favor with the person, and that person will make people respect you based on your position with them.

First Joseph became a father to Pharaoh, and Pharaoh listened to everything that he said. Then Joseph became a lord over Pharaoh's entire house, so Pharaoh's entire house bowed down to Joseph. And then Joseph became the ruler of all of Egypt. In other words, all of his stuff that is in Egypt was under the hand of Joseph. Then Joseph could make a transfer, and Pharaoh approved it based on

Joseph's position and honored him in doing it because Pharaoh trusted him. We need to understand when God deals with a prophet; God gives the prophet his name and calls anyone who stands in the office of the prophet a man of God.

Quit talking and write down your goals. God sent you to nourish somebody. This is the reason that we must go through these seasons. If you don't mind my putting it this way, somebody needs to drink from your spiritual breast to get nourishment, and somebody needs to drink from the oxygen of your attention. I was listening to a man of God who gave this quote from Bishop Jakes.
He was at a conference and Bishop Jakes said that some of us need not allow people to breathe on the oxygen of your attention. You keep things alive because people breathe the attention that you give them; some things will die if we don't give attention to them. Somebody needs to breathe the oxygen of your attention. Church members, if you simply come here and hear this Word, you can breathe from the oxygen of my attention because there is a breathing, living organism here that is going to cause the very thing that you think is dead in your life to live.

CHAPTER FIVE

Sowing Reveals The Heart

Looking at Mark 14, I want to talk with you on how sowing reveals the heart. We have been talking about some amazing things as we have studied the Joseph Principle: being prosperously effective for the purpose of vision, having provisions on the inside of us, and manifesting something for the glory of God. As we begin to look at this, we need to make sure that our hearts are in line with the Word.

Do you realize that giving, or sowing, reveals our hearts? If I sow well enough and make my sowing known to you, I will get a response because sowing reveals the heart. Sowing is our making a particular deposit. Sowing is our taking our money, which we call seed, planting it in the ground, or planting it in somebody's life. When we plant that seed into somebody's life, when we sow seed into the church, and when we sow seed into our lives, there is a revelation about somebody's heart, because somebody is going to have something to say regarding what you sow.

We need to take a good look at this, because as we begin to understand the principle of sowing we must understand that we are going to sow in different ways. Regardless of how you sow, I need to be able to appreciate how you sow. When I begin to sow, you need to be able to appreciate how I sow. We are going to look at a few people and begin to examine several different hearts, and then you are going to have the opportunity to evaluate your heart to make sure your heart warrants God doing for you what you asked him to do.

Remember, it is not necessarily the size of your gift but the condition of your heart that God looks at when you sow.

Mark 14:3-9 shows how sowing reveals the heart, “And being in Bethany in the house of Simon the leper, as he sat at meat, there came a woman having an alabaster box of ointment of spikenard very precious; and she brake the box, and poured it on his head. And there were some that had indignation within themselves, and said, Why was this waste of the ointment made? For it might have been sold for more than three hundred pence, and have been given to the poor. And they murmured against her. And Jesus said, Let her alone; why trouble you her? she hath wrought a good work on me. For ye have the poor with you always, and whensoever ye will ye may do them good: but me ye have not always. She hath done what she could: she is come a forehand to anoint my body to the burying. Verily I say unto you, Wheresoever this gospel shall be preached throughout the whole world, this also that she hath done shall be spoken of for a memorial of her.”

This is a tremendous story because we missed a lot of people who are represented in this story and therefore missed the opportunity to see hearts revealed. What kind of heart do you have? The good news is that God can clean up any heart that is willing to be cleaned.

I don’t want you to miss the flow of what we have been talking about. We have talked about vision and merging. We talked from a business standpoint as well as from an individual or a marital standpoint. For example, when two people get married, they unite forces.

We magnify people's faults and people's weaknesses so much that we miss the awesomeness about their strength, and whenever you unite forces in a marriage or in business situations you always maximize on the strength of the one who you are uniting with. So we talked about it from that point. We talked about merging, we dealt with the uniting of the forces, we dealt with stewardship being a good steward over what God has entrusted to us, and we talked about manifesting the goals that you have set and writing down your five goals that you are believing God for—your goals for the next five to seven years of your life.

Many people have no clue about what goals they have for the next five to seven years of their lives. Guess what? If you don't have any goals set for the next five to seven years of your life, you are going nowhere. You will be on the same dead-end job, and you will be doing the same thing that you are doing today. I was not born with a Bible in my hand. I was on the same corner that a lot of other folks have been on, but there came a time when I had to sever relationships with my boys or even today I would still be shooting craps on the corner. Or I would have still been on the lottery line trying to win another $290. I would have still been right there. I would have still be sucking up everything from beer to grain alcohol. I would still be doing it—I mean, just give me a drink. But at some point I had to come up with goals. Where are you going during the next five to seven years of your life?

Where are you going? What do you predict will happen in your life over the next five to seven years? When we are managers of words, we can say this, "I know exactly what is going to happen over the next five to seven years of my life." Now you go ahead and mock me because I am going to put it out there: over the next five to seven years of my life I will possess my first million dollars.

Look around at all of the people who are in the church; as you see, it is not going to come from this. I just want to make sure because sometimes we can psych ourselves out. I am going to say it like John said it: I am a brother in tribulation like you. In other words, the same way you get yours, I am going to get mine—by believing for it. It is going to come the same way.

I used the same principles in order to get from $326 disability insurance a month to get where I am right now. It took some believing, but you are going to have to do more than believing. You are going to have to put some principles to work that come right from the Word of God. A lot of us are sitting back on our seats doing nothing and waiting for God to do something. But the last time I checked, God was in heaven sitting down. When he came to earth, instructions came with him, and the instructions were that he was going to be a helper to you and me. No wonder the Book of Deuteronomy said "I give to you power to get wealth, I give you ability to get it."

Let's see if we can really get this, because then we talked about the Joseph Principles, the principles that Joseph lived by. If you are going to come to the financial status that God intended, it may mean that fast food may not be in your budget. Look at yourself and say, "Self make some sacrifices so that you can go where you are trying to go." Come up with creative ideas. How many of you have children or someone else living with you? How many of you are responsible for paying the bills of that house? Come up with creative ideas to get everyone to turn off the lights. If the lights are left on, at the end of that billing cycle you are going to have to pay for those left on lights.

How much could we save if the lights are turned off when they are not being used? How can we get the kids to shut the lights off? Are you going to pay an extra $50 at the end of the month if they don't? I wonder if creating an allowance for them would do it and inasmuch as the bill is over budget, subtract from their allowance so that they get to feel the results of the lights being left on.

That falls in line with what we talked about with the Joseph Principle because with the Joseph Principle we talked about the gatherers, those who lay up or store or make deposits or those that guard or keep the stuff. If I am going to be pinching off the money on my way to the bank, then I don't need to be the one to make the deposit. Look at yourself and say, "Self, the pincher cannot deposit." And then there is also someone to keep or guard the stuff; somebody who does not have the gift of giving should be the one to guard the stuff. In other words, let me give you a better understanding of this, you don't ask a fox to guard the hen house.

A good story that I heard some time ago was from the church I came from. They were trying to build the church. In the community where they were trying to put the church, a very lucrative business was copper. One of our businesses was hustling copper taken from around the edges of school roofs and church roofs and taking it to a place called "Rags and Bags" to sell it. Now at this particular church that I was eventually a part of (not at that particular time but eventually I became a part of the church) they were trying to build the church, but the heathens in the hood came and stole the copper off the roof by the time they got back. They couldn't keep anybody at the church, and every time they replaced the copper, it would be gone again. So they got smart about it. This only works in the hood. They found out who the top cats were in the hood and who the top dog was.

The church hired the top dog in the hood to police the area and make sure nobody stole the copper, and they finished building the church. So we set in place guards around that which we are trying to save, because if a people have the gift of giving, guess what? Those individuals are not going to save it because they are going to be moved by compassion, and they are going to give all of the stuff away, and you are going to be broke tomorrow because you put someone to guard the finances that had the gift of giving. So your guard cannot have the gift of giving. Every time someone calls on the phone selling something, look to the one who controls the cash flow that goes out. That individual who answers the phone cannot be someone who would say yes to everyone who calls on the phone to sell something. Look at yourself and say, "Self learn to say 'no' or you are going to have some broke days."

Your heart's condition will determine whether or not God is going to be able to trust you with anything. Your heart's condition will determine whether or not you are even going to be positioned to receive what you are believing for. Look at yourself and say, "Self, I am believing for something." Now we are going to have to deal with our heart to make sure we receive what we are believing for. Here Jesus is in Bethany in the house of Simon the leper, but there are a lot of other people in the house with him and a lot of other people who are represented. Let's study the heart conditions of several of these people because your heart condition is going to determine what God can do for you and what he can't do for you. Even God can't do some things for us, but the heart's condition is going to determine it.

In the house of Simon we had Simon the leper, the woman, Jesus, the disciples, the poor who were outside of the house, Mary, and Martha.
We'll also check some extra verses because in order to see everybody who was in the house, we are going to have to look at the situation from several views. We will refer to Mark 14:3, Matthew 26:6, and John 12:1. When we get this we are going to understand that the heart will determine whether or not you receive or whether or not you will be overlooked.

As we look at this, here we have Jesus in the house, and this woman pours on Jesus' head an ointment that was very costly. The disciples became indignant about what she was doing right here because what she was pouring cost a lot of money. Now we are talking about probably around 15 A.D. and this particular bottle of oil cost $51, and $51 back in that day was a lot of money. And so understanding that it was that much, the disciples become indignant with the woman; because she poured this oil on the head of Jesus. They called it a waste. Now we probably would have done the same thing because of the cost of the oil, but Judas says we could have sold this oil and given to the poor, the Bible says, not that he cared anything about the poor. The heart of Judas was being revealed.

There are several things that happen here; there is no way that Jesus could ever be introduced to the crucifiers without Judas. He needed Judas in order to introduce him. Regardless of whether he was going to be introduced to the world or whether he was going to be introduced to crucifiers, the Messiah had to be introduced. This brings us into a great place for change because he had to be introduced. He had to have a forerunner to be introduced to the world, and he had to have a forerunner to be introduced to the crucifiers. So the heart of Judas was

revealed, the hearts of the disciples were revealed because they got indignant, and the heart of this woman is revealed because she said, “Look, this bottle of oil is nothing compared to who is here.”
Three words describe everybody that was present there in that room. The three words are need, greed, and destiny. As we look at our present situation when we run to the Savior, are you with him because of need, greed, or destiny? Exactly why did we show up for the Savior—to meet the Savior? Exactly why did all of these people end up in the same room with the Savior? Was it need? Was it greed? Or was it destiny? Was it a call of destiny, or did they have a need, or were they just greedy? All three of these reasons could have caused them to show up in this room with the Savior. Isn’t it amazing that all three of these things—need, greed, or destiny—could cause people with different kinds of hearts to show up in this room with the Savior?

The first thing about this is in Mark 14:3, where they were eating at the leper’s house. This is a bad situation. A leper doesn’t mean much to us because we have never met one, and we have heard very little about one, but no one should have been around the lepers, because leprous people were contagious people. But Jesus showed up at the leper’s house, and all of the people who showed up at the leper’s house with him were need, greed, or destiny folks. There were poor people there, people who had tremendous need. There were also greedy people; the disciples had a level of greed—Judas was absolutely greedy because he said that this oil could have been sold and given to the poor. The Bible says he said that only because he was the one who carried the bag, he was the accountant and was stealing out of the bag, and so quite naturally he wanted all of that to be in the bag. On the one hand, the only reason that he was there was because he was supposed to be there with Jesus, but now on the other hand he became indignant was because this was $51 that he wasn't going to be able to get his hands on.

And so the woman poured the oil on the head of Jesus, and Judas, rather than looking at the oil on Jesus' head, paid more attention to what was on the floor and said, "This is a waste." Do you look more on what has been poured on the head, or do you look at what is on the floor? Think about this. Your child comes into the kitchen, goes into the refrigerator, pulls out the milk, and pours her own milk. Isn't that great that she took the time to pour her own milk instead of disturbing you to ask for you to pour it? But she poured too much in the glass, leaving the glass full but creating a mess. Now you pay more attention to the mess instead of the milk in her glass. That is the way we are. Now I am going to ask you again about the condition of your heart. Does it describe need, greed, or destiny? We clobbered the child because she spilled some milk instead of praising her initiative.

Now we will focus on those who showed up and had great need. Jesus wanted to meet the need, but now on the other hand there were other things that were unable to be accomplished. Go with me to Luke 7:44, which reads, "And he turned to the woman, and said unto Simon, Seest thou this woman?" Simon himself became indignant about what was wasted. You see, it was a custom that if a great man came to your house, you were to wash his feet. That was a custom of that day, but Simon didn't even wash the feet of Jesus. Understand this, how can the Messiah, the Healer, go into the house of a leper and leave and Simon still be a leper? Because, that is not what he did. If Jesus came to your house, you can believe that your situation would have changed if he really came. But now he went to this leper's house entered the leper's house and the leper was still a leper when he left. You know why—his heart's condition. I know he didn't have the oil, but if he had only been happy because the oil was poured, he would have been healed.

Understand this. If you can just learn to get happy for somebody, stuff will come to you. We have to share benefits here; yes, she was benefited because she had the oil, but guess what? I can share in her benefit if I praise her because she had the oil. I didn't have the money to give, but I praise God that you did, and I am going to share in your victory. Look at yourself and say, "Self, just be happy." The problem is that your actions reveal your heart. When jealousy creeps up, it starts to reveal your heart, and then you are locked out from receiving because of your heart. This woman had a heart of destiny because destiny says, it doesn't matter what this is going to cost me. I know my heart. My heart is towards destiny, and it doesn't matter what it is going to cost me. I am going to give what I need to give because a destiny is at stake. When destiny is at stake, you get desperate. All of these folks had Jesus in the house, and Jesus was hard to come by.

Go to Mark 14:7, where Jesus says, "For ye have the poor with you always, and whensoever ye will ye may do them good; but me ye have not always." Anytime we are destiny-conscious, we start to have a different approach because we have to sow quickly. You could sow a good enough seed, and it is going to reveal the heart of yourself. Look at the major disturbance that is going to happen based on your seed, that is, the attention you will arouse because you are sowing good seed. An offering causes major disturbances. This woman's offering caused a major disturbance because when she gave she gave $51 over 2000 years ago. It is difficult for some of us to give $51 today. Some of us scream and cry and holler like a baby if we have to give $51 today, but she gave $51 in that day. In 1950 they said $51 was a lot of money, so let's carry it back 2000 years from that point. How long did it take her to come up with $51?

I believe that we can compare that to $1,000,000, and she just gave it up. She just poured it on his head, and the disciples became indignant. Jesus strongly rebuked them, and then you know what happened in Mark 14:10, "And Judas Iscariot, one of the twelve, went unto the chief priests, to betray him unto them." Judas was so messed up and so indignant about what Jesus did that he turned him in to be crucified, and said, "Look, I may not get the money from out of that bag with the $51 it could have been sold for, but I am going to get the money from the high priest and turn you in." It revealed a heart of greed. After he did that offense to the Messiah, a spirit of grief came on him because of what he did, and he hung himself because he could not be freed from the grief. The Bible says that the disciples were indignant based on what this woman did. Judas ran off to turn him in to be crucified, but the rest of the disciples just received the rebuke and changed.

I want to ask you a question about the condition of your heart. If you were rebuked today, would you change your mind according to the order, or would you just get messed up about it and go and try to turn somebody in? The condition of your heart will determine whether or not God could actually do for you what you asked him to do. Lift your hands up and say, "Lord, change me from the inside out in Jesus' name." When destiny is at stake, God says that we shift our whole life from the pleasant status to the status that we have been believing for. In addition to that, he says that when we get there we cannot be found with this mindset, so we have to change our mindset so that when we get there we know how to be millionaires, when we get there we know how to be anointed, and when we get there we know how to be what he called us to be. Look at yourself and say, "Self, I am changing my mindset."

When you change your mindset, there is nothing that the Devil can do to get in the way of the stuff that God has prepared for you. There is nothing that the Devil can do because you don't leave him room. When you open the door for the Devil, the Devil comes in based on the fact that we opened the door for him, but when you know how to manage the people, the finances, and the words, there is no room for the Devil to come in. I want you to look at the God who is inside you saying, "With me all things are possible." Look at the God who is inside you, not the "you" who woke up this morning. When we read the Book of John, we understand that when God sent the Holy Ghost in the earth, he wanted us to rely on the Holy Ghost. He didn't want you relying on yourself. So our understanding comes from the Holy Ghost, our revelation comes from the Holy Ghost, and everything that you have comes from the Holy Ghost.

When we begin to rely on the Holy Ghost, there is an anointing that says that regardless of the situation, that situations can change based on the anointing that is within me. God deposits the anointing right inside you and me. When we gave this demonstration to a class at Bishop RS Walker Ministries, we shared with them that one of the mistakes that we make is when we try to lay hands on folks at a distance. It doesn't matter how badly you are sweating; nothing matters because the person who comes is supposed to be desperate. When you have been before the Lord, everything on you is anointed; I am saturated with the anointing, so I don't stand off from the person because all of me is saturated with the anointing. When I step up to the person and get ready to release the anointing and touch the person, there is a release that comes through my body onto him, and so everything about him becomes affected by what has just come off me.

How about when you get to believing God about something—are you releasing this thing in the earth or is it in the Holy Ghost inside you? We will have problems with this, we will be troubled about this, but when we make contact with the Holy Ghost that is on the inside, then that thing comes quickly. We have learned to let him do it and not do it ourselves. This is not the work of a man or woman; it is the work of the Holy Ghost. When God anoints you for finances, you are anointed even if you don't feel anything. Don't you dare wait on a feeling because the Holy Ghost is not waiting on your feelings? If you are anointed to transact business, when you step into the office the mind ought to change on that man when you step into his presence. Why? Because you didn't step—the Holy Ghost did. I prophesy to you today, my God there is a release for finances in this house today; there is a release for business deals this week. If you have a business deal next week, see if you can move it up into this week when the anointing is on it. I don't care if it is something as little as just going to look for a job, go after it, but go after it with the anointing on you.

Look at yourself and say, "I am anointed for increase, I am anointed to work this next deal. I am anointed to receive this next measure of my first million." Let me ask you a question. How many of you have a business deal that you have to work this week? If you are, this thing is going to bring about an absolute manifestation this week if you can believe it is done. Here is the thing that the Holy Ghost wanted me to say: if any of you are delinquent in your tithing, this is not going to work until you come up to date in your tithing. Now being delinquent in my tithing says that there is a condition in my heart that is like the heart of Judas, I have been stealing out of the bag. How long does it take to repent from being a thief? The Bible gives instructions on how to get yourself redeemed because you borrowed the tithe. This is so serious before God because you go into this place of change. Now I want to speak a Word and when I speak this Word to you I want you to receive it, I want you to absolutely receive it.

CHAPTER SIX

Receiver Types

It is very important for us to understand that we can't afford most of what God will send us after. We see no way that we can get it. If we see that we can get, then we don't have to exercise our faith—it puts no pressure on our faith. If I can measure my stuff to get a fancy car, then I really don't need God to get it. But if my stuff does not measure out to be enough, then I need God to show up. But more important than having God show up, I need to know how to "believe in" the stuff so I can get it. This becomes extremely important for us to understand. We see what we are going after, then we learn how to believe the stuff in because it is going to take money on hand to get what we are after. How do we believe the money in to match the price of what we want? This is where we have to be consistent if we are going to move up on exactly what God is trying to get to us. You don't measure what you are after according to what you see. You have to measure it by the Word.

We can develop a level of understanding to improve our hearing so that our hearts will be able to produce according to what we hear. Let me say that again: if we are going to get what we are after, our hearts have to produce the faith to get it. In Mark 4, if we can get to the point where we really understand this, then even the sky isn't a limit to what you can have. This is not just a material thing. This is a principle that we are talking about that goes right across the board. So for every single thing that we desire from the Lord, we believe that thing in. First, deal with your heart because it is going to be your heart that is going to produce what you need. Everything you have in the earth right now your heart has produced, be it positive or negative.

Even if it is failure, your heart produced it. Guard your heart with all diligence, for out of it, the Bible says, are the issues of life. Everything flows from your heart, so your heart can produce whatever it believes.

Let's understand this. We are talking about principles, we are talking about laws, and we are talking about specific laws that govern the earth. Once we understand that there are specific laws that govern the earth, then we can understand how we get particular things to happen in the earth. The process is this: I hear the Word, I meditate upon what I heard, it goes down into my heart, it is stored, and once my heart understands it and it is stored in my spirit, my heart becomes flooded with it, my mouth speaks it forth, and the earth gets hold of my words and begins to produce what my words were in the earth. This is the process by which we get the earth to produce for us.

There are two ears that are listening to see what will be produced for you as an individual. First, the Devil is listening; his ears are listening to hear what you are giving him permission to produce for you. Second, God is listening to hear what you are giving him permission to produce for you. The Devil feeds off negative words and fear; fear is to the Devil is like faith is to God. The Devil can't work off your faith because faith works against the plans of the Devil. But fear works against the plans of God for our lives. Faith works in such a way that God hears what you said, and then he is able to do what you said because it was mixed with faith. When the Devil hears faith-filled words, he becomes intimidated because the words move against everything that he stands for. When God hears fear-filled

words, then the words move against God. God is never going to be intimidated, but fear-filled words move against God, so God can't do anything for you.
As we think about that, we can understand why Jesus had gotten to the point where he had to hit the disciples pretty hard verbally when they started operating in fear and unbelief when they were on the boat in the storm (Mark 4:37-41). He had to hit them hard because people's lives were at stake and what they were literally saying was going to give the Devil every opportunity to make the storm work. So Jesus scolded them for having no faith. They were in the midst of a storm, and Jesus expected that after all that he talked to them about, their words would be different.

God is looking for every one of us not to fear under pressure. When you get fearful under pressure, your heart starts to produce fear and it starts to produce everything that fear produces. When our words are so filled with fear, they produce doubt and unbelief—it fills the room, it fills the earth, it fills wherever you start speaking with doubt and unbelief, so that will be the product based on what you said.

Go to Mark 4:14-20, which reads, "The sower soweth the word. And these are they by the way side, where the word is sown; but when they have heard, Satan cometh immediately, and taketh away the word that was sown in their hearts. And these are they likewise which are sown on stony ground; who, when they have heard the word, immediately receive it with gladness; And have no root in themselves, and so endure but for a time: afterward, when affliction or persecution ariseth for the word's sake, immediately they are offended. And these are they which are sown among thorns; such as hear the word, And the

cares of this world, and the deceitfulness of riches, and the lusts of other things entering in, choke the word, and it becometh unfruitful. And these are they which are sown on good ground; such as hear the word, and receive it, and bring forth fruit, some thirtyfold, some sixty, and some an hundred."
This becomes important; every one of them had the Word in common. And since they all heard the Word, every last one of them had the potential to produce thirtyfold, sixtyfold, or a hundredfold. Every last one of them had the potential to produce that. But the problem occurred when they all didn't hear it the same way and didn't do the same thing with the Word that they heard.

When you hear the Word, what do you do with it? This is the real question, because every one of us can get the same results from the Word. This goes right across the line. Every single thing that the Word produced for one person it will produce for someone else, but it depends on how we use what we have heard.

Look at yourself and say, "Self, there are no limitations in God." And since there are no limitations in God, there are no limitations in us. We limit ourselves based on how we hear. How do we hear the Word? We limit ourselves on that. For example, it was the Word that I had to use in order to come up out of alcohol, in order to come up out of drugs, in order to come up out of everything else. I had to work the Word against what I was bound with.

For getting particular things that I wanted, I had to use the same Word that I used to come up out of drugs and alcohol. I used the same Word in order to get what I desired to have. It is all a matter of how you work the Word. And you know what? Here is the challenging thing about it. You never get to the place where you don't have to use the Word every time a test comes. Tests always come; they never stop. But we outgrow how we got started. This is the major problem with us as people; we outgrow the way we got started, as if reaching a certain age or point with God means we can use another process. You don't use another process. It is the same process.

We end up growing up in the things of God and then starting to fail, because we think we can change the process because we have been with the Lord all this time. No, the process doesn't change. You go right back through the same process, and you will realize that this is a law, this is a principle that governs the earth, and therefore you use this same process over and over again.

You will begin to use greater levels of the Word in order to produce greater levels of things that you desire in your heart. In Mark 4:14-15, look at how a few of these different people heard. "The sower soweth the word. And these are they by the way side, where the word is sown; but when they have heard, Satan cometh immediately, and taketh away the word that was sown in their hearts." Satan came immediately to this bunch and took away the Word that was sown in their hearts. It was sown in their hearts, but Satan came immediately to get it, and they gave it up. Why? This particular bunch on the wayside heard the Word as they were sitting beside you in church and as soon as they walked out of the door, a strong wind came and that Word was gone, so it did them no good. But how they heard the Word and to what measure they held onto that Word was up to them.

Many people come to church every week but never hold onto what they hear. Think about yourself and what you would say if I asked you, "What did we talk about last week?" Do you realize that very few people can tell me the majority of what we talked about? Are you a wayside hearer? Are you one of those who allow Satan to snatch the Word immediately from them? Mark 4:16 reads, "And these are they likewise which are sown on stony ground; who, when they have heard the word, immediately receive it with gladness;" They were glad that they heard the Word, and they received it with gladness, and it had no root in themselves. Look, the Word doesn't go deep into them at all, as in Mark 4:17, "and so endure but for a time," only for a little while they endured with what they heard. Continuing in the same verse, we read, "...afterward, when affliction or persecution ariseth for the word's sake, immediately they are offended." This is the bunch that gets offended. Did you notice that it didn't say that Satan came immediately with this group? You know what comes? Trouble comes, offenses come, and they receive the offense just as quickly as they receive the Word. You see, nobody can make you mad. Somebody presents you with an opportunity, you jump on it, and you get mad. That is how it happens. And guess what the Devil was after all the time—the Word that was sown in your heart.

Look at yourself and say, "Self, don't get offended." You have to decide not to get offended. I make decisions like this all the time. I have all kinds of opportunities to get offended, but I decided that I'm not going to get offended because I can't afford it. Why? I will never forget the Greek word for offense, "scandelon," because it means that there is a scandal on that is after my Word, and I can't afford that. When somebody does something to you, even though the natural response is to be offended, you can decide not be offended. When somebody starts whispering and the first thing you do is become offended, you can't afford it.

Mark 4:16 begins, "And these are they likewise which are sown on stony ground; who, when they have heard the word, immediately receive it...." That is the first step, receiving what you heard. But guess what is going to happen if you receive what you heard and you let that Word stay inside? Guess what it is going to grow up and become? The Devil can't let it stay in there, but guess what? He doesn't have authority over whether or not the Word stays in there—you do. To try to get that Word, he sends an offense any way he can.

Once people are offended, they will cough up that Word. No, it's not coming up that easily; that is like trying to vomit up something that is already digested. No, that is not going to happen. But the offense comes after what you heard that is working. The offense doesn't come unless you have received the Word that you heard. The strategy of the Enemy is not to let you get further than that first step that you just took. What did you do? Step one, you heard the Word. Step two, you received it, and you didn't just receive it, you received it with gladness. But then right on the other side of your gladness came the offense.

Maybe that has never happened to any of you, getting glad about what you have heard. We rejoice over that Word, and then the next day, if not that night, somebody makes you mad enough to smack him or her and then have a nice sleep. But the objective of the Devil right there has nothing to do with you and has nothing to do with how anointed you are. The Devil isn't even thinking about that. The only thing that he wants to make sure of is that God's Word does not take root any deeper than it has already gone. You received the Word with gladness, but after the offense you coughed one time, and out came that Word. And that is all that the Devil ever wanted.

Here is the thing that we don't do. We never associate that offense with the Word that we received yesterday or last week; we don't associate the two. We think, "That doesn't have anything to do with it." It has everything to do with it. I am showing it to you right here. What in the world does an offense have to do with God's Word coming to you? Remember the sower sows the Word, but you are the ground that receives the Word. Mark 4:18-19 reads, "And these are they which are sown among thorns; such as hear the word, And the cares of this world, and the deceitfulness of riches, and the lust of other things entering in, choke the word, and it becomes unfruitful."

Guess what? It didn't happen to this hearer—well, wait a minute; it actually did take root to a degree because this one didn't cough it up. The thing we have to see in this is that what happened to the two hearers was different. The previous hearer coughed it up and the Word came out, but the Word never came out of this hearer. The Word was still in there, but the cares of this world, the deceitfulness of riches, and the lust of other things entered in because the Word wouldn't come out.

All by itself the Word is productive, so all God has to do is speak a Word to us, so we can get that Word inside us and guard that Word so that nothing can attack that Word. Do you understand that Word is coming to pass, as surely as your name is what it is? So this one hearer didn't cough it up. This one didn't get offended, so the Devil had to try something else with this one. He had to move this hearer to a point where he would operate under the cares of this world, the deceitfulness of riches, being deceitful about how he was going to get money, and the lust of other things in case he didn't care about the things of the world. He didn't get tripped up by money but by the lust of other things. Or maybe the lust of other things didn't even come into play; maybe he couldn't care less about anything in the world but the deceitfulness of riches. All of these worldly cares choke the Word, and the Word becomes unfruitful. It is not automatically unfruitful; it is being fruitful when it gets in there. It starts a process of producing something, but the worldly cares act as a weed does, growing around the plant until it chokes the life from the plant. Was the plant producing? Yes, it was producing, but the weed came in and choked the plant, causing the plant to become unfruitful.

Once the Word enters in you, it starts a process of producing in you. But when we get off track on the cares of this world—the deceitfulness of riches, and the lust of other things—where do the cares of the world enter into you? In the same place the Word entered, the heart. Worldly cares get hold of the Word and begin to choke it, and the Word that had started producing becomes unfruitful. When I started to understand this, I started to watch very closely when I believed God for something. You are supposed to believe God for something; that is when the stuff starts happening. How do you dare talk about what you are believing God for? Watch the test come. It will start at ground level first to see if it can snatch the Word that was sown in your heart. If it can't snatch the Word you are holding onto tightly, the Devil tests you to offend you. If the Devil has thrown everything that he can throw at you and you won't even get offended, he brings temptations before your face and brings the cares of the world and deceitfulness of riches to your mind. Then the Devil sees if he can get you involved with the lust of things like cars. The temptations could be anything, even lusting after food. Guess what happens? The lust goes in, it chokes the Word, and the Word becomes unproductive. You might not lust after a woman or a man, but the Devil doesn't care because the Bible didn't specifically say that lusting after a man or a woman enters in and chokes the Word. The Bible said lust enters in and chokes the Word.

When we worry about only one type of lust, we don't guard ourselves against those other areas. And then the principle of the thing turns on, and then we start to fail in our process of what we were believing for. What do we have to do? We have to keep our minds and attention focused on not doing anything excessively. The man that you feed the most will be the one who will win. Let me ask you this: when you can have something that you absolutely love to eat, does there ever come a time in your life when you decide to exercise discipline instead of eating when you have a pocket full of money? Somebody might say, "I think I am going to fast today." Fasting might not be your choice if you don't have money or haven't brought a lunch. Please don't get me wrong; that is good time to take an opportunity like that. If you don't have any money, you can't eat, so you might as well get the benefit of not eating today.

When we go to a buffet, what are we doing? We are exercising discipline so that this lust for food doesn't ever get an advantage on us. We go to the buffet and say, "Jesus, I am going to make a decision right now. Instead of getting those five plates of food that I usually get, I am going to get a half of a plate today." Here is where we are working our discipline and keeping our flesh under subjection especially when we know that the Devil is getting ready to drive this thing right home. The cares of the world, the deceitfulness of riches, and the lust of other things enter in for one reason: to choke that Word that you embraced and didn't cough up.

Look at Mark 4:20, "And these are they which are sown on good ground; such as hear the word," number one, "and receive it," number two, and "bring forth fruit," number three." I am telling you how to believe this stuff in. It comes in according to how we believe it in, according to the degree to which we believe. Remember that in the first step, we heard the Word.

In the second step, we received this Word. And when we received it we went through the process and broke down the process of really getting this thing in our heart and not our spirit so that our heart would be flooded with it. The Bible says that from the abundance of the heart the mouth speaks. Once the mouth speaks into this world, God hears exactly what you said, and the angels are ministering spirits sent forth to minister for them who shall be heirs of salvation—heirs of salvation, heirs of deliverance, heirs who have full rights to everything that Jesus had rights to because he purchased it all for us. And since he purchased all of that for us, this thing is turned on, and this is one of the important reasons why we have to be hearing this and go through this whole process of receiving the Word.

The third step was to bring forth fruit by believing the Word and responding to the Word with a corresponding action. When you take a corresponding action according to what you heard, you know that you really believed it, and your actions will show up according to what you heard. For example, every one of you believes that the chair that you are sitting in right now will hold you up. So you flopped into the chair because you were positive that it was going to hold you up. Why? Maybe you were tired, but you also had a present confidence based on a past experience. The chair supported you before, so you had confidence about sitting in it. What if the last chair that you sat in had collapsed and landed you right on the floor, and the chair before that put you right on the floor, and the chair before that put you right on the floor? You are going to check out the next chair really well before you sit down because in front of all the people around you, you are not going to want to land on the floor. But because that didn't happen, you have a present confidence based on a past experience.

When was the last time that God moved out of the way and let you fall? He hasn't done that, so we ought to have a present confidence based on the fact that he has held us up time after time. Therefore, we ought to be able to receive it just because he said it. Here is how we produce. Don't ever worry if you have only produced a little. The fact is that you produced—some thirtyfold, some sixtyfold, some a hundredfold. So what if the guy down the street, or the sister down the street, produced at a hundredfold and you only produced at thirtyfold or tenfold? You produced.

What do we do the next time? We follow it up with more consistency, more sticking to the Word, more believing faster than we believed last time. And this time we are going to produce thirtyfold or maybe even sixty-fold or maybe even a hundredfold, but we are going to produce at a different level now. And this is exactly how we get it. We can get it every single time. You can get it every single time that you work the Word, and the only thing that we are going to have to do is get back up and do it again.

Remember that the degree to which you receive will be the degree of your harvest. A harvest manifested has only manifested to the degree that you actually received it. So what do we do? We work on ourselves because we are absolutely determined we are going to shoot for a hundredfold. What is a hundredfold? It is one hundred times. We are shooting for a hundred, and since we are shooting for a hundred now I would rather shoot for a hundred and get half of it then shoot for ten and get all of it. What I am saying is aim high. Shoot to get the bull's-eye.

And if you shoot to hit the bull's-eye and fall on fifty, praise God because you produced fifty according to your receiving.

We must understand this because God is ready to meet our needs. I was talking to people the other day who were making a deal on getting a house financed. As I understand it, it was their first house. They had sat down with a person, developed a relationship with the person, and started to work out the plans together for this house that they were doing. This person was asking them when they were going for their next house, and their thought process was let us get through this one first, and then we can talk about the next one; once we get this one, then we will think about the next one. But now wait a minute—consider how God thinks.

Aim high; God doesn't wait until you are in your harvest before he starts talking to you about the next one, but if your thinking is not there, then he won't talk to you about the next one while you are finalizing the first one. You have to get your thinking to the place where while you are finalizing your present deal you are thinking ahead about the next deal. Some will call that greed, but I have a plan for a harvest that God could look down on and cause him to say to me, "Well done, thou good and faithful servant."

I meditate upon my harvest. We have to think that way, because when we march into our harvest we ought to already know what the next harvest is going to be. Please, let's not have such small thinking that we can't meditate upon another deal while finalizing this one. But if this is your first deal, don't let the Devil trick you focusing on two deals at the same time. Don't let the Devil to cause you to have divided focus, or you won't get either one. Remember, this is your first deal, so we are finalizing this one, and now that we are at the table finalizing this one, our thinking has already run to the next deal, the next one we are going to buy. Let's thank God for the Word. God has already started a process to develop things on the inside of us and to give us things, but we have to have our receiver open. Have your receiver wide open.

CHAPTER SEVEN

Receiving From Faith Versus Fear

When we read Mark 4 and start to understand the different types of hearers, let's look at them again, this time considering the thought process of faith versus fear so we can talk about receiving from faith versus fear. You are going to receive things based upon either your operation of faith or your operation of fear.

We get the opportunity to use either one. It is up to us which one we are going to work. You can work faith or you can work fear. If you are going to work faith, then you are going to produce the results of faith. If you are going to work fear, then you are going to produce the results of fear. Operating in faith is going to cause faith stuff to be attracted to us, while operating in fear is going to cause fear stuff to be attracted to us. You are the kind of magnet or the kind of repellant that you operate. You are going to draw to you whatever is operating in you, or you are a repellant to the opposite of what you have operating in you. Nothing comes to you that is recognized as faith stuff if fear is operating in you; you turn out to be a type of repellant that wards off all faith stuff from even coming to you. This is something that we have to understand because it is not going to come just because we love the Lord. It is going to come based on what we are working. If we learn to work the Word by using our faith, then faith stuff is attracted to us, and we repel the fear stuff. Fear stuff will stay away from us whenever faith is present.

Let's go back through here and see if we can nail it down based on that, in Mark 4:14-15, "The sower soweth the word.

And these are they by the way side, where the word is sown; but when they have heard, Satan cometh immediately, and taketh away the word that was sown in their hearts." If fear were operating in this particular hearer, the sower soweth the Word, and these are there by the wayside where the Word was sown, but when it was sown, Satan came immediately to take out the Word that was sown in their heart. Even though they heard the Word, fear was the dominant force that was operating in them, so much that they feared that they would lose stuff. If you start to fear that you are going to lose something, just stay tuned because you are going to lose it. Why? You are going to lose it because faith is working in the negative—that is called fear. However, when faith is working, then the fear stuff doesn't become a dominant force around you.

Read Mark 4:16-17, "And these are they likewise which are sown on stony ground; who, when they have heard the word, immediately receive it with gladness; And have no root in themselves, and so endure but for a time: afterward, when affliction or persecution arises for the word's sake, immediately they are offended." This offense shows up and steals stuff that is in their hearts.

In Colossians, this becomes extremely important. Now they have no root in themselves and endure only awhile because they have no root in themselves. Colossians 1:15-23 says, "Who is the image of the invisible God, the firstborn of every creature: For by him were all things created that are in heaven, and that are in earth, visible and invisible, whether they be thrones, or dominions, or principalities, or powers: all things were created by him, and for him: And he is before all things, and by him all things consist. And he is the head of the body, the church: who is the beginning, the firstborn from the dead; that in all things he might have the preeminence.

For it pleased the Father that in him should all fulness dwell; And, having made peace through the blood of his cross, by him to reconcile all things unto himself; by him, I say, whether they be things in earth, or things in heaven. And you, that were sometimes alienated and enemies in your mind by wicked works, yet now hath he reconciled In the body of his flesh through death, to present you holy and unblameable and unreproveable in his sight: if ye continue in the faith grounded and settled, and be not moved away from the hope of the gospel, which ye have heard, and which was preached to every creature which is under heaven; whereof I Paul am made a minister."

Let's look again at the last part of that passage, verse 23, "If ye continue in the faith grounded and settled, and be not moved away from the hope of the gospel…,"or the hope of the good news; this is what that hearer didn't have. He wasn't rooted, grounded, or settled, and we believers need to be rooted if are going to operate in faith. You are going to have to be rooted, grounded, and settled in the Word. A lot of us don't spend enough time in the Word to be rooted, grounded, and settled in the Word. Read Colossians 2:5-7, "For though I be absent in the flesh, yet am I with you in the spirit, joying and beholding your order, and the stedfastness of your faith in Christ. As ye have therefore received Christ Jesus the Lord, so walk ye in him: Rooted and built up in him, and stablished in the faith, as ye have been taught, abounding therein with thanksgiving."

We can't just ignore these instructions. Colossians 1:23 teaches us what we need to be: rooted, grounded, and settled. Many of us don't reach the point of being rooted, grounded, and settled. But when we start believing God for something,

we have to get to the place where we are rooted, grounded, and settled in the thing that we believe for or else we can't have it.
Most of us are not willing to put in the work that it is going to take to get it. Just because you read it one time, or just because you asked and you know the scripture that says if I believe I receive then I have it that is not going to get it right there. That is not enough. Read Mark 11:23-24, "For verily I say unto you, That whosoever shall say unto this mountain, Be thou removed, and be thou cast into the sea; and shall not doubt in his heart, but shall believe that those things which he saith shall come to pass; he shall have whatever he saith. Therefore I say unto you, what things soever ye desire, when ye pray, believe that ye receive them, and ye shall have them."

Believe that you receive them and you shall have them—we don't see the process of becoming rooted, grounded, and settled in the thing, then receiving. Their belief is one thing; receiving it is something else, because you believe it there and you believe it in. You don't settle for anything else because if you are rooted, grounded, and settled in the thing, then that is the thing that you are impregnated with. Look, you are so impregnated with that that, you are not even seeing anything else. Some people won't understand you and will get mad at you and ask why you are so stuck on your goal. You will be focused because this is where your faith is, and you will be so zeroed in on that thing inside yourself that you would not be able to imagine yourself moving. You will be rooted, grounded, and settled on it.

Read Colossians 2:5-7, starting with verse 5, "For though I be absent in the flesh, yet am I with you in the spirit, joying and beholding your order, and the

stedfastness of your faith in Christ." Now I'm seeing this; I am beholding your order and your steadfastness in your faith in Christ.
Read verses 6-7, "As ye have therefore received Christ Jesus the Lord, so walk ye in him: Rooted and built up in him, and stablished in the faith, as ye have been taught, abounding therein with thanksgiving."

How do you believe for salvation? Here is a big problem: we think that salvation comes one way and that what we believe for comes another way. But that is not at all true. The way that you believe for salvation is the same way that you believe for healing, for deliverance, for a house, for a car—it is the same way. Once we understand this principle, then we move to a place where we can believe anything in. Read Romans 10:8, "But what saith it? The word is nigh thee, even in thy mouth, and in thy heart: that is, the word of faith, which we preach…"

This is important. The Word—which is the same Word that we preach, the Word of faith—is near you, even in your mouth and in your heart. It is not a different Word; it is the same Word. And he is saying that the Word that we preach is near you, even in your mouth and in your heart. The same Word that we preach came into your mouth, and it came into your heart, and that is the Word that you are going to believe—if thou shalt what? Read Romans 10:9, "That if thou shalt confess with thy mouth the Lord Jesus, and shalt believe in thine heart that God hath raised him from the dead, thou shalt be saved."

If you believe in the process, if you believe in the Lord Jesus and the components of the principle, then you have the very object that you went after. But let's go back for the principle; I don't want you to get caught up on Jesus being the object of the faith right now. I want you to see the principle of it. Now it says in Romans 10:8-9, "But what saith it? The word is nigh thee, even in thy mouth, and in thy heart: that is, the word of faith, which we preach; That if thou shalt confess…" Now you have the Word in your mouth and in your heart, but it can't lie dormant in your mouth and heart. The next phase is that we have to confess it. We are going to have to speak it. We are going to have say something. You are not going to be able to possess the thing and not declare or confess the thing that you say you possess in your heart. If you confess with your mouth and believe with your heart that God has raised Jesus from the dead, then you will have what you are after: salvation.

Let's review the components of the principle again. The first component is in Mark 4:14-15, where the sower sows the Word. We start out with the Word, and we receive the Word in our hearts and mouths, according to Romans 10:8. Then in Romans 10:9, we need to highlight the words, "confess," "believe," and "thou shalt be saved." So first we deal the Word because we need the Word in order to manifest this. Second, we "confess" it. Third, we "believe." And fourth, we believe that "thou shalt be saved." These are components of the principle that we need to get into our spirit.

If what we believe for is not manifesting, then we need to go back to one of those components and see it. Review Colossians 1:23 so we can learn how to handle what we just got hold of. "If ye continue in the faith grounded and settled, and be not moved away." Being grounded and settled is going to take some level of tenacity because it is easy to be distracted. If you are not grounded, rooted, and settled, just being under pressure will move you away from your focus. If you are not grounded, rooted, and settled, you are going to be moved, so do whatever it

takes for you to become grounded, rooted, and settled in the thing. If you know what you believe for, that is your position, and you are not going to be moved if you are deeply grounded, rooted, and settled.
Colossians 2:5 reads, "For though I be absent in the flesh, yet am I with you in the spirit, joying and beholding your order, and the stedfastness of your faith in Christ." What quality of faith in Christ? The steadfastness, unmoving faith in Christ. Now that is the kind of stuff you just need to sit down and take a break and think about. In other words, we are not being moved off our faith anymore. Let's read further. Colossians 2:6 reads, "As ye have therefore received Christ Jesus the Lord, so walk ye in him." Now this will get you, won't it? That very first word—"as"—in other words walk in the same way in which you have received Christ Jesus the Lord.

They just got right up out of their seats, didn't they? They said, "I receive Jesus as my Lord and my Savior," and they walked back to their seats and said, "I am saved." You know that was a persuasion that they had, just because they came up here and received him, just as easily as that. God has not made this thing difficult at all—we have made it difficult. He instructs us, "As ye have therefore received Christ Jesus the Lord, so walk ye in him." Okay, next verse—but wait a minute. How are we walking in him? Colossians 2:7-8 tells us, "Rooted and built up in him, and stablished in the faith, as ye have been taught, abounding therein with thanksgiving. Beware lest any man spoil you through philosophy and vain deceit, after the tradition of men, after the rudiments of the world, and not after Christ."

This is how the Devil got our roots dug up, through traditions of men, through good-sounding stuff, through stuff that just seems to make sense but is wrong. Now that we have tapped into all of that—rudiments of the world, traditions of men—here is what we have to do. We have to remember what God said. What did God say? Where are we going? We are going right back to the first thing—the Word, and we are not moving off of the Word.

Hebrews 12:1, says, "Wherefore seeing we also are compassed about with so great a cloud of witnesses, let us lay aside every weight…" What are we doing here? We are laying aside every weight because now the Enemy is looking for opportunity, right? Remember what we were talking about at first. We started by talking about the different kinds of hearers. The Enemy used things around the hearers to get their attention off the Word because they all heard the Word. The Enemy will do anything to get your attention off the Word. He will use television to get our minds off the Word, he will use people to get our minds off the Word, and he will use all kinds of interesting things to get our minds off the Word. Here you are in the Word, and a sandwich will pop up in your thinking, right in the midst of a good study, and you think, yeah, I think I have that right down in the refrigerator, right? And then you think about how you can eat while you are studying your Bible.

You don't need to eat when you are studying the Word. Right in the very midst of getting a revelation is when your thinking is diverted to something else, something that has nothing to do with the Word. When you are diverted, what you are literally saying is, "God, hold that thought. I will be right back," as if what he is saying is less important than what you are getting ready to get out of the refrigerator. Well, now God doesn't want to talk. So watch this. At this point the only thing that you are going to get is what you can come up with yourself. Look at yourself and say, "Self, what could be more important than you hearing the Word?"

What could be more important than hearing the Word at that particular point? God is going to reveal things to us, but we can't put God on hold.
That is the reason that when he wakes us up in the middle of the night, we don't need to go back to sleep. God wakes us up at three o'clock in the morning. He wants us to rest because he understands how important rest is. But when he wakes us he has something to say. And then we humiliate him by going right back to sleep. He would have said the same thing if we had just sat up in the bed; we didn't have to get out of the bed and down on our knees before he was able to speak. No, the only thing he needed was our attention. God is not religious at all. He doesn't need us on our knees. Our knees don't have anything to do with what he is saying. I believe it was Elisha who was listening to God, and he put his head between his legs and God still spoke. God would have spoken if his head hadn't been between his legs.

Again, Hebrews 12:1 says, "Wherefore seeing we also are compassed about with so great a cloud of witnesses, let us lay aside every weight and the sin…" Not just the sin, but what? Not just the sin but every weight or anything that weighs you down and prevents you from hearing God. Look, if the cookie in the refrigerator prevents me from hearing God, do you know what I am not going to do? I don't care how much I love cookies. I'm not going to the refrigerator because I need to hear what he has to say. I know the results of putting God on hold; when I wanted to hear him later, he wouldn't say what he would have said before I put him on hold. I know what it is like to roll over, go back to sleep, wake up and ask, "Lord, what were you getting ready to say?" and hear that heaven is silent. And I follow God's ways myself. I say that if you are not going to listen to me when I am talking, I am not going to say it later. Where do you think I learned that statement? I got that from God. I tell you, God will do that in

a minute if you think sleep is more important than what he has to say. He is not going to speak to you when you wake up. If he does, you had better cut a step really quickly in your bedroom because that is not the norm for God.
Maybe you say that you are believing God for a car. That has to be rooted and grounded in you, because if you can get to the point where you are not moved off it, then manifestation will happen. That is how God sees your faith. He sees that you are not moving and are steadfast on this thing, so he has to manifest this thing in the earth. Consider Hebrews 12:1 again, "…let us lay aside every weight, and the sin which doth so easily beset us, and let us run with patience the race that is set before us." You don't have to run fast. You run with patience. Look at yourself and say, "Self, you don't have to run fast; just run with patience."

Then you have to let patience have its perfect work. We have to experience things so patience can have its perfect work in us. Our desires are not going to happen because we read a scripture and find the promise. It is not going to happen that way. Hebrews 12:2 begins, "Looking unto Jesus the author and finisher…" Jesus authored your faith and he finished it. So if we are going to have what we are looking for; we are going to have to let him author it, and we are going to have to let him finish it. If he authored it, then he gets to call the shots on this, and you follow his process, not your own process. You go right back to the Word.

You know what? I can tell you stories that will curl all of our hair forever. I can tell you some stuff that I had to believe for that you would be embarrassed to talk about in public, stuff that I had to believe for that I didn't want to tell anybody, and God came through. I said, "God this is your Word. This, right here, is your

Word to me. You are the author and the finisher of this." I tell you, this is the way that I had to talk to God while I was believing for something. You have to stand firm with this; you don't just stand up there looking all cute and say, "Lord, you know your Word says faith is substance of things hoped for."
No. Say, "God, you said you are the author and the finisher of my faith, and my faith right now needs help." You have stuff on you that you didn't cause or see coming. Say, "God, you said a thousand shall fall at your side and ten thousand at your right hand but it shall not come high thee. You said that this wouldn't come near me, God; look, here is your Word."

Now what if everybody is turning you down? Say, "God, you said that if I desire anything according to your will you will hear me, and if I know that you heard me, then I know that I have the petition that I desired of you. Well, God, I know you heard me." You know what this does? God sees you as an individual not wavering but, rather, being rooted, grounded, and settled in this thing, and he says, "I have to manifest this because this believer is repeating my Word."

Let's finish Hebrews 12:2, which starts, "Looking unto Jesus the author and finisher of our faith…."You are looking unto Jesus, not at anything else. He is not only the Word; he is the author and the finisher. So you are looking at the author and finisher. Nothing else matters. Continuing, we read, "…who for the joy that was set before him endured the cross, despising the shame…"of having not fulfilled it. Now that makes a difference doesn't it? Despising the shame of having not fulfilled it. God bragged that you would make it through this, and now we have to despise the shame of having not made it through. Look at yourself and say, "Self, I am a finisher and I finish strong." Some of you won't remember this, but there was an advertising commercial that was on a long time ago that said, "I would rather fight than switch." This is the concept that we have to adopt: I would rather fight than switch off what I am believing for.

In James 1:2 we read, "My brethren, count it all joy when you fall into divers temptations; Knowing this, that the trying of your faith worketh patience."
Unless your faith is tried, it is not faith yet. Real faith can stand the test. We like to avoid having our faith tested. Lord Jesus, I just don't believe that I have to go through this. But I am going to have to endure this because my faith needs to be proven as faith. So the pressure comes on to see if it is really faith. Maybe I will go ahead and coin the phrase, "Is it faith or is it fake?" If it is really faith, then when it goes through the trying period, it comes out gold. If it is not faith, it comes out burned. Remember that works will be burned if they are wood, hay, or stubble? (1 Corinthians 3:12-15) When a person's work goes through the fire, if it is really not faith it comes out burned up, but if it is really faith it comes out as pure gold tried in the fire. If it is really not fake, it will stand the test and you don't have to worry. It is going to make it through because it is really faith. Your flesh might not make it through, but your faith is going to make it through right along with your spirit. The test is what determines whether or not it was faith or fake. Your storm will determine whether it is really faith. This is not determined by you or me. Let's just receive seed; is it faith or is it fake? Just go ahead like the eagle. The eagle runs ahead into the storm. It doesn't turn around and go back the other way because it sees a storm coming.

CHAPTER EIGHT

Natural Words, Supernatural Faith

Mark 11:12-15 reads, "And on the morrow, when they were come from Bethany, he was hungry: and seeing the fig tree afar off having leaves, he came, if haply he might find anything thereon: and when he came to it, he found nothing but leaves; for the time of figs was not yet. And Jesus answered and said unto it, No man eat fruit of thee hereafter forever. And his disciples heard it. And they come to Jerusalem: and Jesus went into the temple, and began to cast out them that sold and bought in the temple."

Let's back up just a little bit and read, "And they come to Jerusalem: and Jesus went into the temple, and began to cast out them that sold and bought in the temple." Let's make sure we understand that. "…and seeing the fig tree afar off having leaves, he came, if haply he might find anything thereon: and when he came to it, he found nothing but leaves; for the time of figs was not yet." Verse 14 becomes important, so let's read this very slowly, "And Jesus answered and said unto it…" he said to the tree. What is the object? The object is the tree, right? Read, "No man eat fruit of thee hereafter forever." When he says the key words "here after forever"—in other words, from this point on nobody will eat fruit of this tree—what do you think he was expecting in this? This is exactly what we do when we start believing for something. The Devil sends us on journeys running after things that are not there. The tree was the object, not the figs; the object of his speaking was the tree, and so if nobody was going to eat fruit of the tree from this point on, then what do you think he was actually

looking for now? He was looking for the tree to die because it was nonproductive; it had no fruit on it even though it had leaves.
Do you like math, or are you at least familiar with math and word problems? Do word problems draw your attention to everything else except for what the deal is? It's the same in this tree example. You focused on the fact that it is not time for figs, you focused on the leaves, you focused on everything except for the tree, and that is exactly what the Devil does to us every time we go to believe for something. We go after everything else except for what the real deal really is. And so what is the real deal? It is not time for figs, but he walks up to this tree and it only has leaves on it. If it had leaves on it, it should have had fruit, but it didn't because it was not time for figs. The objective of Jesus was to teach the disciples something based on what the tree didn't have.

We have to understand that Jesus understood his assignment. When Jesus pulled up his disciples, he started a process of teaching them. When did that process end? It ended at the crucifixion. The process of teaching them was not just when he put them on the hill. When he walked up to that tree, he was teaching his disciples that if the only thing that you are is a tree with leaves and have no fruit, you are worthless, and if your faith does nothing else other than make loud sounds, it is worthless. It has got to do something more than just make noise. It has to produce something. He said to the tree, "…no man eat fruit of thee hereafter forever." He was looking for that tree to dry up.

There is something else that we need to see here. Jesus walked off, never giving that tree any more attention. He didn't have to come back by to see if it did what he said. He knew that words went out to accomplish what he was saying. In

Mark 16:19-20, we read, “So then after the Lord had spoken unto them, he was received up into heaven, and sat on the right hand of God.
And they went forth and preached everywhere, the Lord working with them, and confirming the word with signs following.” What was he going to confirm? He was going to confirm the Word. When Jesus spoke in the earth, what do you think that God was going to confirm? His Word—when the words flowed from the mouth of Jesus, God was under obligation to confirm those words. The words went out and the object was the tree, so that tree had to die and dry up and pass from this earth. Why? It had to die because Jesus spoke words to that tree.

Let’s say for instance now here you are believing God to provide something. You heard the Word and repeated it. What should you be expecting? You should be expecting that to come to pass. See if you really believe what it was that you said. Let’s look back at our example setter, Jesus, in Mark 11:14. “And Jesus answered and said unto it, no man eat fruit of thee hereafter forever. And his disciples heard it. And they came to Jerusalem and Jesus went into the temple and began to cast them out…” Now what was Jesus doing at this point? He was moving on about his business because he left his Word back there to work. Either you are going to work or your words will. But we have to liberate our words to work for us. How do you liberate your words to work for you? You have to leave them alone. You can’t stand there, being concerned with how this situation is going to come out if you really believe. Read on a little further. He went on about his business and in Mark 11:20, “And in the morning, as they passed by…” They had left the tree, and verse 15 says they came to Jerusalem—they turned around. Jesus was teaching them something. Jesus knew what was going to happen before he left the tree. He was teaching them and took them by the tree, not as if he was taking them to show them the tree, but just walking back the same way

that they came. Mark 11:20-21 continues, "And in the morning, as they passed by, they saw the fig tree dried up from the roots.
Peter calling to remembrance saith unto him..." Peter called to remembrance what? Mark 11:21-22 finishes, "Saith unto him, Master, behold the fig tree which thou cursedest is withered away. And Jesus answering saith unto them, Have faith in God." Peter remembered that Jesus had cursed the tree and noticed that it was dead, and Jesus said, no big deal, have faith in God—in other words, have the God kind of faith.

What does that really mean? That when God said, "Let there be light," he expected light to be turned on. I wonder how many of us expect what we say to come to pass. We ought to expect it to come to pass, but do we really expect this? Let's find out if you really expect what you say to come to pass. How many of you still use negative words to express yourself? Are you still working on getting some of those negative words out of your vocabulary, yet you still use the negative words to express yourself? If so, you might not really believe that what you say will come to pass. What if you were to say, "I don't have any money." If you were to say that to someone, what that says is you don't believe that what you say will come to pass. Your words perpetuate your status. If you verbalize the idea that you don't have anything, you are actually speaking into the earth what is not and the thing that is not becomes not, or I should say the thing that is becomes not.

Read in Romans 4:17, "(As it is written, I have made thee a father of many nations,) before him whom he believed, even God, who quickeneth the dead, and calleth those things which be not as though they were." He called those things that are not as though they were. That is how they came into being. Now flip the script.

If you are already seeing something that is not, but in the realm of the spirit it is, then you are canceling it out the minute you say it based on what you see in the natural world. You are perpetuating what is not already in the earth so that it never comes from the realm of the spirit into the natural.

Let's read the verse above one more time. God quickens the dead, he makes alive the dead, something that is no more, "And calleth those things which be not as though they were." Then he calls those things that are not in the natural world, and then they come into the natural world based on what he said. When he created the world, the earth, Genesis 1:1 says, "In the beginning God created the heaven and the earth. And the earth was without form, and void; and darkness was upon the face of the deep." There were no lights on and it was empty—that was the status of the earth. Is it full today? Billions of people are here now, but nobody was here then. He said, light be, and the lights turned on. He called light into the earth when light wasn't here, so he called that which was not as if it were.

When we understand that what we say comes into being, we need to watch what we say. Even in our joking moments we must watch what we say because everything that we say comes to be. Here is something that we say, "Well you know the Lord knows I was just kidding." But wait a minute; God doesn't play with words. The minute something is verbalized, the first process of making something happen is already in the system. This earth is designed to hear words in order to manifest what is in the mind of the God man. Psalms 8:4-5 says, "What is man, that thou art mindful of him? And the son of man, that thou visitest him? For thou hast made him a little lower than the angels, and hast crowned him with glory and honour." But here is the point: David wanted to know why God is mindful of man. Here is what man is—man is a portrait of what God is.

Let's go back over it in Genesis 1:26, "…let us make man in our image, after our likeness: and let them have dominion…." Now if man has dominion and dominion is carried out through his words, in the same way, God carried it out through the words that he was speaking. Now if he carried it out through the words that he was speaking, then he expected man to have dominion the same way. When you have dominion, your very words command a response from somebody.

God speaks a thing and it is. God says a thing and it comes into manifestation. Therefore, if God made you in his likeness and after his image, then when you say something, it comes into being and manifestation. But there is one gigantic problem: Now you have to value words in the same way in which God values his Word. Here is the value that God puts on his Word: I will exalt my Word above my name. Most of us don't feel that way; most of us will exalt our name above our words. But God is on a whole different system. Remember, at the name every knee is going to bow and every tongue is going to confess, and he says he will exalt his Word above that. If that's the way that God feels about his words, how can we just throw anything out there in words and then say that we believe that the words will come to pass? So now we have to pay a lot of attention to our words because the Devil is under obligation to obey my words inasmuch as I obey my words. All of the elements in the earth are under obligation to obey your words inasmuch as you obey your words, or to honor your words in as much as you honor them.

This takes some practice. We are not going to readily commit to a whole bunch of things; neither are we going to minimize what we say to make it easy on ourselves.

You don't speak less to make it easy on yourself; neither do you say just anything that you know you are not going to honor. Here is an example from my own life. One night I received a phone call reminding me about an invitation to attend a graduation the next day. But the next morning I looked at my caller ID, saw that the call had come in, and realized I had never heard my phone. I was so tired that morning, it was not funny. I'm telling you, I was whipped. I lay there and thought, "Oh, God, I am too tired to go," but then the next thing I faced was, "Rodney, you said you would go," so regardless of any tiredness I got ready to go because my word was out there. The graduating person probably would have excused me, but I wouldn't excuse myself because my words were out. So that became my driving point. Tiredness will make you back out on commitments that you say if your words are not that important to you.

This is something that I had to work on, making excuses like, "They just need to understand." No, you need to understand that if the Devil can get you to the point where you don't value what comes out of your mouth, then he doesn't have to pay any attention to what you are saying. How about one of the Ten Commandments, thou shall not take the Lord's name in vain? In other words, you should not use the Lord's name in vain because if we have no more value of that name of Jesus than to just throw that name around, then when it is time to use it, it won't work.

When I was a kid we used to like to watch Dracula movies. We didn't have to go to a party because we just flipped on television on a Friday night and watched Dracula. But there is also a Dracula comedy now, one of the stupidest Dracula pictures I have ever seen in my life. In the regular Dracula movies, if a person put up the cross, then Dracula backed up. But in the Dracula comedy, the person threw up the cross and Dracula just laughed and jumped on him and bit him; Dracula paid no attention to the cross.

The cross had no value in this particular setting. And today if the cross has no value to you, if the name has no value to you, if your words have no value to you, the Devil will do exactly the same thing. He will ignore your words when you put the name of Jesus behind them. He will slap you with the sickness anyway until we come to the point of saying, man; this right here is the Word of God.

When somebody asks you a question, do you claim the Word of God, or do your own ideas and your own worldly thinking come out? People—even Christians—will tell you not to answer them with a Bible answer but to talk to them straight. But are you kidding? Tell them that this is what you learned to live from; this is how you got healed. Ask them where the answers should come from, if not from the Bible. Tell them that they wouldn't want an answer from you that is not based on the Word. Line everything up on the Word so when we start believing for something then it is not difficult to get results based on what you are believing for. You want to make sure that everything that you have done up to this point has been based on the Word. You have already been in the Word. Then based on the Word you stop speaking death and fear words and learn to fill your mouth with faith words, words of life, and words that are going to bring life. And then it comes down to your very own words. You reach the point where you stop using dead stuff to express yourself. When it comes down to your word, you value your word. So even if you say, Lord Jesus, I really don't feel like it right now, and I'm tired from what I am going through right now, you still go and do exactly what it is you said you were going to do. You will see your words working. Even when you are joking around and stating the truth, make sure that even the truth doesn't make reference to death or fear stuff because we are not trying to get those kinds of results.

How important are your words? Let's review the Book of Mark again to finish up. Jesus used words against this tree, but remember that Jesus came down as mere man with the Holy Ghost in him so his words weren't any more powerful than our words. His being Jesus didn't make his words any stronger than ours, but what put the power behind his words is that he began to govern what he would say and then he got filled up on God's words. Because he understood how words work in the world, his words had power. He used ordinary words in Mark 11:14, "No man eat fruit of thee hereafter forever." There is nothing holy or powerful about those words. Those are regular dictionary words. You don't have to go to a biblical dictionary to find those words. In Mark 11:22, he says, have faith in God, or have the God kind of faith that now does something about the natural words that you speak. He used natural words with supernatural faith, and the faith boosted the power of those words and made the words supernatural. And calleth those things which be not as though they were, he says, "For verily I say unto you, that whosoever shall say…" now this makes more sense to us. Everything that we just talked about is what Jesus understood right up front. Remember he said in Matthew 12:36 that you shall give an account of every idle word that you speak.

I like what Kenneth Copeland says about this word system. He says that Jesus Christ is the high priest of God's Word, yet he is Lord over all words. He is Lord over every single negative word that the Devil or anybody else will speak to you. He is Lord over those words, but he is high priest over his own words, high priest over every Word of God, which means that he carries that Word and causes that Word to be carried out in the earth. We have to govern the words that come out of our mouths because we are going to bring a manifestation in the earth according to the words that we speak. Now this is the reason we can have what we say so we have the God kind of faith working on the inside of us to put some "super" on the natural words that we are speaking.

Then Mark 11:23 means more to us, "For verily I say unto you, That whosoever shall say unto this mountain, Be thou removed, and be thou cast into the sea; and shall not doubt in his heart, but shall believe that those things which he saith shall come to pass, he shall have whatsoever he saith." He shall have whatever he saith, and you will have whatever you say. As long as you can see what you say, not in this natural world, you get a mental picture of that which you are praying for, and then you start verbalizing the picture because it is real to you. Remember, Jesus had a mental picture. Before he walked away from that tree, he already knew what was going to happen to that tree; the disciples were the ones who didn't have a mental picture of it. Therefore, they had to recall what he said 24 hours prior. They had to recall these words in their tomorrow because they had no mental picture yesterday.

You can grab these words right now and create a mental picture for your tomorrow so that when you step into your tomorrow, you are not surprised when manifestation happens. Why? You had the picture yesterday. People will think that you are boastful, proud, arrogant, and all of that because when it actually happened you were not the one who went dancing and jumping all around up and down the aisles. They didn't see that you rejoiced yesterday when you saw the picture. If you really saw what you should have seen yesterday, then you rejoiced yesterday. So when tomorrow comes, you have already formulated a picture in your mind about your particular tomorrow.

Matthew 12:36 says, "But I say unto you, That every idle word that men shall speak, they shall give account thereof in the day of judgment." Every idle word shall men give an account.

You put a lot of words out there, and somebody has to give an account of those words because a lot of stuff was created that possibly should have never been created. And now God wants to know who created all of this stuff that was not created by him or through him.

What about "true" versus "truth"? It is true that I have symptoms of a cold, but the truth is that by his stripes I am healed. So I understand that in saying that, we are not to say that we don't have money. For example, if you ask me for money to help with something, and I have money but my money is budgeted for my bills or other purposes, I am not going to rob Peter to pay Paul. So technically I don't have the money, but the truth is I know that I am rich and all that the Word says, but what do I tell you? I can't lie and say that I don't have the money. Or would you say that I should admit that I have the money, and by saying that, I am believing it in so I would be able to give that to help you out?

Well, that is a good question, but it is not going to go well with my natural mind, because when I am walking in faith, I don't necessarily owe anybody an explanation. Secondly, if I am going to say something, then I will just say that I don't have that in my budget right now. For instance, we have three stores. We have a bookstore, a clothing store, and a food store. If they are going to operate properly and independently, then we shouldn't take money from the clothing store to put food in the food store. Food money is budgeted for food, clothing store profits are budgeted only for clothes, and likewise the bookstore budgets for books. If the bookstore has an overflow right now, and the food store is running short, it might seem logical to borrow $1,000 from the bookstore. The bookstore says $1,000 is not in the budget right now, but in its account there is $1,000,000. But that amount is in their overflow; their budget can't afford $1,000.

If you have a savings account and you have a checking account, the checking account is to pay the bills and the saving account is what you are storing up. When the checking account goes all the way down to zero, then you have that savings account. What if somebody wants to borrow $1,000 and you have $50,000 in that savings account? The truth of the matter is you really do have the $1,000, but it is not in the budget because reaching into savings would interrupt your savings plan. So that $1,000 is not in your budget to give. It is almost as if that money really doesn't exist, and it doesn't exist for this purpose. And so now if I don't presently have the money in any accounts, any pockets, anywhere, then I'm still not going to say I don't have it. I can be creative with what I say, but I refuse to say I don't have it, because I don't want those words to be manifested in the earth.

Let me give you an example in the story from 2 Kings 4:8-37. Remember when Elisha, the man of God, prophesied to a Shunammite woman that she would bear a son, and later the son died? After her son died, she said she was going to go and find the man of God, and her husband asked, "Wherefore wilt thou go to him today? it is neither new moon, nor sabbath." She answered, "It shall be well." Even though her son was in a room dead, she refused to say that he was dead; instead, her words were, "It shall be well." There wasn't anything well, so this might seem untruthful, but the truth to her was, God, you gave me that boy and this is not the end of this process. But it would have been the end if she had said it. The boy would have slipped off into paradise (and I am saying paradise because it was before the resurrection of Jesus) if she had said, "He is dead," but she wouldn't declare that. So when she found Elisha, the man of God, and he asked her if all was well, she again said that it was well. Now that is calling something there.

How was her son going to be raised from the dead if she didn't tell the man of God, who could raise him from the dead, about her son's death? That is faith. She refused to let death conquer her son in a day when death hadn't been conquered yet. She refused to let death conquer her son because she conceived her son based on a word from the man of God.

Now, how are you going to creatively say what you need to say so that you are still in faith? You have to come up with something that is not a lie, because a lie isn't going to work either. It can't be a lie because God is not going to be glorified through your lie.

Some people debate with me about whether joking is appropriate. "I joke a lot, and I know a lot of people do, too. But I am trying to really understand the power of my words and joking because some things are extremely funny. Let's say someone runs up the stairs, trips, and falls. Come on, that is funny, and I might look at it and say, if it is funny, it's just funny. How do you help not making it a bad thing? In our choir rehearsals, numerous things can happen, and we all understand it is fun and games. And I know you are saying when we joke with the truth that we are joking with the Word, and all that the Devil needs is a word to go on, but how do you know how to separate that? Because you know I am really trying, but I am not doing that well at it." Well, there is a difference between reality and a joke that hasn't happened, because when someone trips and falls, that is something that actually happened and could have been serious.

"What about jokes about being a short person? So are we saying that speaking that is saying that you are short? Because I have heard people tell me that, and I tell them, no, you are not going to grow anymore." This is where the rubber really meets the road.
Okay, yes, that may be true, but we may refer to that without really saying that specifically. Using death or fear words will come under that because with some people, I may do some short person jokes, but I will only do that if I don't really think they have a complex about being short. If you have a complex and might be offended, you will never ever get that joke out of me. "Okay, then what is the difference?" Based on their response, you will know whether or not the person has a complex.

"I guess I am bringing this up because I want you to leave me alone and let me crack my jokes. If it is not a death word, leave me alone. If you find it funny, laugh. If you don't find it funny, don't laugh. Because what you are saying now is that the appropriateness and power of my words depends on the person with whom I'm joking."

That is true. Someone might want to tell a tall joke about me, and that's fine with me. That is true about me, but with these words, now we have a relationship. So if you say something about me and it is true, if I don't have a complex in that area we can go there, but the very second that I or you detect that there is a complex, then you really have to back off because now it has changed from fun and truths to fun and death for that person. There are a lot of things that I don't joke about, because especially when you don't know the person I don't think it is tasteful to make jokes just for the sake of making jokes. You don't know who is within the sound range of your voice that is hearing and then becomes offended.

You know what? We changed something in our church's vision based on the fact that it offended somebody. I don't remember what we said, but we rephrased it. There was a white lady in our service one time, and when we talked about "every kind reaching its own kind," she got offended and asked if we were prejudiced, so I changed it. It is still the vision, but we reworded it so that it did not sound offensive, because that vision is not an offensive thing. The vision has nothing to do with color. For example, if I don't know Spanish, it is better for me to teach in English to a Spanish-speaking person who understands English and then let that person go to the whole Spanish nation? Then I need to learn to say a couple of things to witness to them in Spanish. No, instead, let's start a process to make sure we are teaching all of these different folks, and they can go to the people in their own language and dialect. That is what we mean in our vision statement. But because the person was offended by the previous version of the statement, we reworded it so that it wouldn't be offensive. You have to be attentive because if you are not attentive, you keep on verbalizing things that may hurt people, and you don't know your words are hurting them because you are not attentive. If you pay attention, then you will be able to see people's sensitivities and not offend them.

About the Author

"Jeremiah 1:9-10 (KJV) 9 Then the LORD put forth his hand, and touched my mouth. And the LORD said unto me, Behold, I have put my words in thy mouth. 10 See, I have this day set thee over the Nations and over the kingdoms, to root out, and to pull down, and to destroy, and to throw down, to build, and to plant.

Bishop Rodney S. Walker I is a dynamic prophetic voice whose ministry is renowned as being a catalytic agent for understanding and maturing in the prophetic. A native of Washington, D.C., Bishop Walker is the Founder and Senior Pastor of Heritage Church International, established in 1990 in Waldorf, Maryland. He serves as the General Overseer of Bishop R. S. Walker Ministries - formerly Another Touch of Glory Ministries - that covers national and international churches, para-church ministries and businesses. He is spiritually covered by and accountable to Dr. Michael Freeman of Spirit of Faith Christian Center in Temple Hills, Maryland. He is also submitted to his Spiritual Father, Bishop Ralph L. Dennis of Kingdom Fellowship Covenant Ministries in Towson, Maryland. In addition to being a graduate of the Jericho Christian Training College, Bishop R.S. Walker received his Doctor of Divinity degree from The Spirit of Truth Institute.

Bishop R. S. Walker's training by versatile and equipped instructors, guidance from his mentor, as well as submission to his Spiritual Father, has developed him into a well-balanced, grounded, and seasoned prophet. On July 19, 1997, Bishop Walker was ordained Elder in the Office of Prophet by Kingdom Fellowship

Covenant Ministries. In 1999, Bishop Walker founded the School of the Prophets.

The School has locations in Waldorf and Baltimore, MD, Raleigh and Wilson, NC, Abuja, Nigeria, York, Pa, and has been hosted throughout the United States and beyond using online streaming. March 15, 2002, Bishop Walker completed the coursework for the Joint College of African-American Pentecostal Bishops Congress and July 3, 2009 was Ordained and Consecrated in the Office of Bishop by Kingdom Fellowship Covenant Ministries.

In addition to equipping and training in the prophetic, Bishop Walker has also assembled a body of Prophetic Presbyters who assist him in managing the great assignment God has set to his hands.

Bishop Walker is the author and publisher of over 10 books including: *The Prophetic Prayer Journal, Raising Prophets of Character, Becoming a Proven Prophetic Voice, The 21stCentury Prophet, The Renaissance Prophet, and The Father/Son Encounter,* all of which prove to be phenomenal resources of the serious believer's library. Among Bishop Walker's many accomplishments, it is that of being a devoted husband to his lovely wife, Pastor Betty A. Walker and a loving father to his eleven wonderful children.

Bishop Rodney S. Walker's ultimate goal is to fulfill all that God has purposed for his life and to effectively lead those placed in his prophetic and pastoral care. His love for God is evident in his preaching, teaching and zeal for ministry. You will experience the wind of the Spirit through this Man of God.

Order Form

2760 Crain Highway
Waldorf, MD 20601
301- 843-9267 or 877-200-8967 • _F_a_x_ _2_4_0_- 427-4606
www.rswalkerenterprises.com • _e_-mail: admin@bishoprswalker.com

Bishop R.S. Walker

Name ____

Title ____________________ Date ____________________

Church/Ministry ____________________________________

Address ______________ City ____________ State ____ Zip ________

Daytime Phone ________________________ E-mail ________________

Items Ordered:

Description **DVD CD Quantity Total**

Raising Prophets of Character Book $14.95

School of the Prophets 15-week Course $190.00 Discount $110.00

Renaissance Prophet's Manual	$43.95
Foundations of Prophetic Maturity	$15.95
The Art of Tongues Book	$10.00
Raising Prophets of Character Prayer Devotional	$14.99
Creating Habits for a Functional Life	$14.99
The Father Son Encounter	$14.95
The Fundamentals of Faith (6-CDs)	$50.00
The Ministry of the Holy Spirit	$15.95

Shipping Information:
Add $4 for Priority Mail first item
$1 per additional item
MD add 6% sales tax **Method of Payment:**
Please charge my: Discover MasterCard VISA AMEX Card Number:
Expiration Date (Month/Year): / / Signature (as shown on credit card): Check or Money Order
For Speaking Engagements contact: The Administrative Office of Bishop RS Walker Ministries: (240) 573-3418 or admin@bishoprswalker.com

Total price of items --
Add shipping charge ---------------------------------------
Tax (if applicable) ---
Total Amount Enclosed ---------------------

www.ingramcontent.com/pod-product-compliance
Lightning Source LLC
Chambersburg PA
CBHW080513110426
42742CB00017B/3099

* 9 7 8 0 6 9 2 4 9 4 6 1 5 *